MW00710439

What Every Catholic Should Know About the

MILLENNIUM

Christopher M. Bellitto, Ph.D.

Liguori
ONE LIGUORI DRIVE
LIGUORI MO 63057-9999
314.464.2500

Dedication

For Paul, Juliana, Eric, Beth,
and the little ones to come.
The future is theirs.

Imprimi Potest:
Richard Thibodeau, C.SS.R.
Provincial, Denver Province
The Redemptorists

Imprimatur:
Most Reverend Michael J. Sheridan
Auxiliary Bishop, Archdiocese of St. Louis

ISBN 0-7648-0146-5
Library of Congress Catalog Card Number: 97-74319

Cover design by Grady Gunter

Acknowledgments

In the Middle Ages, a scholar named Bernard of Chartres declared he was only able to understand certain religious topics because he was a dwarf standing on the shoulders of giants. This popular work on the history of apocalypticism stands on the shoulders of giants in the fields of history, religion, sociology, and other fields. The anecdotes, examples, and depictions of various eras are drawn from many books and articles, but the style of this little book prevents detailed citations. The list of further reading found on page 60 represents its main sources; I've used endnotes for quotations and especially unique stories or insights. You'll see that I am particularly indebted to the work of Bernard McGinn, the dean of apocalyptic studies in the United States.

This effort, then, doesn't claim to offer new scholarly research. What I hope to accomplish in *What Every Catholic Should Know About the Millennium* is to reap from that mass of scholarly material. My goal has been to present that material in a format which is accessible to the everyday reader and to offer that reader my own reflections. Some of those reflections have been raised in passing by other scholars in the course of their academic publications, but I've run with them freely here. I've tried in my own way to make academic work relevant to our lives as Catholics as we cross the threshold of the third millennium. Otherwise, important scholarly research may remain available only to a small circle. It doesn't belong only there, though, because academic authors have much to teach all of us. This book is an attempt, then, to bridge the gap between the lecture halls of academia and the kitchen tables of our daily lives.

I am also grateful to others who have helped me along the way.

The entire staff of Archbishop Corrigan Memorial Library at Dunwoodie generously assisted with many requests and often joined me in the joy of the acquisitions and research hunt. Kass Dotterweich of Liguori Publications showed an enthusiasm for this project which went even beyond my own from its earliest stages. Her sympathetic ear, sage advice, and careful pen greatly improved the manuscript as she guided it toward publication. My students pressed me for greater clarity and offered their own insights in seminar discussions, presentations, and papers. Some will find echoes of the stories and sources they dug up and mulled over in these pages. I thought I was navigating them through this material, but they pointed out new paths for me to explore, as well.

Finally, I thank my wife, Karen, who read every word of every draft despite working on her graduate studies in the evenings and on weekends. Her candor and constructive criticisms challenged me to keep my audience and purpose in mind on each page. With great patience, diligence, and charity she listened, spoke, and edited. She probably knows more now about apocalypticism than she ever desired, but she accepted this project because it was important to me. I am humbled by her love, support, and faith.

Prologue

Thinking of things to do on New Year's Eve 1999? The fancy
Rainbow Room in New York City is already booked for its New
Year's Eve party and there aren't many seats left on the airplanes
that will fly across time zones and the international date line so
passengers can experience the turning of the millennium twice. Organizers in Great Britain, meanwhile, are looking to train people
to ring every church bell in the country on January 1, 2000. Millennium commissions are springing up in cities and countries across
the globe.

Are you already behind the times? If you haven't signed on for
the big events yet, will you miss anything? Should you be making
any special plans for this historic event? And what does it all mean
anyway? Will it be the End of the world?

Over the past two thousand years, people have spent a great
deal of time and effort trying to figure out when the End of the
world will arrive. Since Jesus ascended into heaven, there have been
many predictions about the Second Coming of Christ and the related arrival of his archenemy, the Antichrist. As early as the first
century, for example, Christians saw the persecutions they suffered
under the Roman Empire as signs that they were being purified in
the last days of the world. A thousand years later, a huge pilgrimage of Christians set out from Germany to be in Jerusalem on Easter Sunday, March 26, 1065 because someone calculated that the
first Easter was on March 26 and concluded that Jesus would naturally come again on such an anniversary. Later in the Middle Ages,
some Christians became convinced that the Antichrist had taken
over the papacy itself. One theologian in the early fifteenth century, checking his astrological tables, predicted that the End would

arrive in 1789, which may have seemed like the End of the world if you were a member of the aristocracy or royal family experiencing the French Revolution. And during the Reformations of the sixteenth century both Catholics and Protestants labeled each other as the Antichrist or his evil helpers.

They were all wrong of course, but mistakes of the past persist. In 1996, a newspaper in suburban New York City decided to note what it called historic events connected with the turning of centuries. Most of the events cited had nothing to do with apocalyptic predictions. For example, the newspaper noted that Marco Polo dictated his memoirs in a Genoa prison cell in 1299; that Shakespeare wrote *Julius Caesar* in 1599 (just three years after the English first ate tomatoes which had previously been considered poisonous); that Russia's progressive czar, Peter the Great, taxed men's beards in 1698; and that a century later, the Rosetta stone proved to be the key to understanding ancient Egyptian hieroglyphics. What do these dates and events have to do with the End of the world? Nothing, but they make good stories, like when the *Washington Post* decided to name Genghis Khan its "Man of the Millennium" in 1995.

So why all the commotion about the Year 2000 anyway? Will it be the End of the world, as some people are already predicting? Does it have any particular meaning for Catholics? What does the Church say about all of the prophecies of doom and gloom? This book will not provide answers to every question nor will it describe each movement in the history of apocalypticism which picked apart the Book of Revelation.

The goal of *What Every Catholic Should Know About the Millennium* will be to help us understand three things: how Christians have dealt with "signs of the End" over the past two thousand years; how the Church officials responded to these prophecies; and how we can use the lessons of the Church's last two millennia to help us prepare well for her third millennium.

The bottom line is this: we don't know when the End will come and there is no special reason to believe that the Year 2000 will have anything to do with Jesus' promised return. No, there is no one clear formula for calculating the End, though people claim to have it. There is no single undisputed outline of people or incidents that can be labeled the final events or signs of the Second Coming, though people have preached them for centuries and offer them today on television or the Internet.

Finally, there is no one authoritative Catholic reading of the Book of Revelation which interprets current events like some divine Nostradamus, though some Catholics will claim to hold the answer—or at least cling to unfounded rumors. For example, the famous "third secret of Fatima" offered by our Lady at the beginning of this century does *not* contain an apocalyptic vision, as many claim. This fact was attested to in 1996 by no less an authority than Joseph Cardinal Ratzinger, prefect of the Congregation for the Doctrine of the Faith and, as a news report put it, "one of the few people in the world who has actually read" the "third secret."[1] Catholics who persist in believing that our Lady—or anyone else for that matter—has accurately predicted the End must be following the advice of the journalism professor who half-jokingly told his students, "Never let the facts get in the way of a good story."

Stated bluntly, spending your time calculating the End is not what we're about as Catholics. Saint Augustine, writing more than 1,500 years ago, warned that trying to figure out the moment when Jesus will come again is a waste of time. Instead, uncertainty grounded in joy, hope, and faith is the rule. It's that simple.

But that doesn't mean we should overlook the End. Even Bernard McGinn, the leading scholar of the history of apocalypticism, says that he has been trying to discover "an approach to Christian eschatology that takes it seriously but not literally."[2] We are, after all, an apocalyptic people—a fancy way of saying that we're waiting for the End and have been ever since Jesus ascended into heaven. McGinn even says that "Christianity was born apocalyptic."[3] Say that with a smile and watch people scrunch their brows in confusion. If that also strikes Catholics as odd, consider that we pray "Thy kingdom come" and proclaim that we wait "in joyful hope for the coming of our Savior, Jesus Christ" in the Our Father at Mass. But these prayers and proclamations don't make us a lunatic fringe.

Why is a review of Church history the best means to discover how waiting for the End should be a normal, mainstream part of Catholicism—but has not always turned out that way? Looking back at the history of the Church is like sitting around the dinner table with old photo albums and reviewing our personal or family histories by telling stories. There are bad times with the good, of course. But it's important to stop at certain key moments and reflect on where we've been. That way, we know who we are and where we're going.

This goal of reviewing the past before moving into the future is precisely why Pope John Paul II declared the Year 2000 a Jubilee year and asked us to spend the years coming up to the turn of the millennium reflecting on our history. He would like Catholics as individuals and the Church as a community to treat the coming of the third millennium as a time of renewal, education, inspiration, and growth. By following John Paul's suggestion, we can calm ourselves of some of the crazy fears that surrounded prophecies of the End in the past—and which increasingly assault us today. We can also use the Church's past to educate ourselves about our family history and gain a deeper understanding of our heritage in general. In particular, we can learn about our very important, and sane, legacy concerning what apocalypticism really means to Catholics. Finally, we can reflect on the past to grow within, to inspire ourselves to embrace that legacy, and to live the positive elements of apocalyptic spirituality that are with us whether it's the Year 2000 or 20,000.

That is why this book was written.

Notes

1. *Catholic News Service*, October 14, 1996.
2. Bernard McGinn, *Antichrist: Two Thousand Years of the Human Fascination with Evil* (San Francisco: HarperSanFrancisco, 1994), p. 2.
3. McGinn, *Visions of the End: Apocalyptic Traditions in the Middle Ages* (New York: Columbia University Press, 1979), p. 11.

Introduction

Some people fear the new millennium. Others have a morbid curiosity or a superstitious giddiness that impels them to go along with the crowd. Then there are those who have no idea what all the fuss is about.

Precisely because members of this last group have no sense that people have worried about the End of the world before, they are likely to follow all the hoopla connected with New Age prophecies; they are subject to being seduced by the literal interpretations of the Book of Revelation which promise an absolutely correct prediction of when the End will occur and what events will take place. People who may be insecure will grab on to such a prophecy of unerring truth without questioning it or realizing they are like sheep blindly following whomever or whatever promises security. Not a few Catholics may be part of this last group, which is why it is important for Catholics to be both countercultural and cultural by anticipating the new millennium with everyone else but doing so with joy, hope, and faith—not fear, dread, and a false sense of security.

Why look for the End anyway? That's a good question with answers that often point to psychological factors.[1] We all want to believe that our lives matter. We want to understand where we fit into the big picture. Playing a part in the Final Judgment surely means that our lives matter. Knowing about the End seems to give us a greater sense of security, maybe even control, of our own lives even when the world appears to be spinning out of control around us.

According to the leading scholars of the history of apocalypticism, many portraits of the events of the End can be categorized as a cycle of crisis-judgment-salvation. If you or your race or your country are in a crisis that you do not understand, you can feel lost. But paint that crisis in cataclysmic terms and all sorts of possibilities open up. You are forced to take a stand nobly: for your people or for surrender, for good or for evil, to fight and perhaps die in glory or to submit in weakness and humiliation. If there is hope that your good efforts will make you worthy of reward, however, you may fight with more conviction and less fear. The promise of salvation, victory, or simply some type of gain will push you forward.

The Sky Is Falling

Despite these lofty goals of apocalyptic spirituality, the truth is that when most people talk about the End they think of things which are, quite frankly, a little crazy—something like Chicken Little running around crying, "The sky is falling! The sky is falling!" We've all been approached by people in the streets declaring, "Repent, the End is near!" In cities like Chicago or Los Angeles, these people are so common they don't even attract attention. What's more, they seldom show up the day after their predictions didn't come true, and if they do show up, it's because they've recalculated their dates and want us to trust them again. This is not new, of course. When predictions of the End didn't come true in the Middle Ages, people just pushed the date forward again and again and again.

One very pushy man came up to me early one morning on the subway as I traveled into New York City to take an exam in college. I had slept only an hour the night before and was extremely worried about that particular final. "The world will end today at 2 p.m.!" the man kept telling me as he shoved a flyer detailing his plan for my salvation in my face. Exhausted and disgusted, I replied, "Can you make it this morning? I've got an exam at noon I know I'm going to blow." He walked away, quickly.

All of this can be charming and funny—until it's not. Much of the imagery, rhetoric, and propaganda surrounding predictions of the End, for example, can be dangerous. Consider the fact that Hitler saw his Nazi regime as a Thousand Year Reich, a traditional length of time related to the peaceful and prosperous reign of Christ in the Second Coming. Politicians have often used this same kind of hype to paint themselves as heroes of the good and their enemies as the forces of the Antichrist. Both United States President Ronald Reagan and Soviet Union President Mikhail Gorbachev were labeled by some as Antichrists: Reagan, because each of his names (Ronald Wilson Reagan) had six letters (666) and Gorbachev, because of the port wine stain on his forehead (two marks of Antichrist for those who believe in such things). When the Branch Davidians were holed up in their Waco, Texas compound against federal authorities, it appears that they saw their predicament as the Final Great Battle between the forces of evil (the United States government) and themselves (the elect). They believed they were a persecuted minority, a belief which fed into their notion of themselves as the chosen few who had to die in glory for their leader. Heaven's Gate followers in California saw the Hale-Bopp comet as the sign of their end in 1997.

We can argue, of course, that these are the rantings of a lunatic fringe or of isolated nut cases, but the lunatic named Hitler murdered six million Jews and must also shoulder his share of responsibility for the deaths of millions of soldiers and civilians in the war he created. In this age of the Internet, instant communication, and tabloid television ready to make a buck by selling garbage to the gullible, the lunatic fringe can quickly seem like the powerful loud majority. At that point, the feeding frenzy of fear rapidly takes over and what ordinarily seems ridiculous begins to appear reasonable.

The Lessons of History

The fact that crazy positions are so scary, available, and accepted is a fundamental reason for Catholics to understand the *history* of apocalypticism. Recently, a person told me I was all wrong about the timing of the End. "You academics think you've got it all figured out," she told me after I'd stressed there was no reason to believe that the Year 2000 had any special significance. But she was adamant. "The world *is* coming to an End. Everything is the worst it's ever been. This is the century of sorrows but more people are coming back to the Church, too. This is *definitely* the End." She was sure that she was right and I was wrong.

If I had wanted to be impolite, I would have told her that she was putting herself above Jesus, who admits that even he does not know when his Father will place power in the hands of his Son (Matthew 24:36 and Mark 13:32), a statement that Scripture scholars connect with the End of the world and the Final Judgment. Jesus himself says that it is not for us to know the time of the End (Acts of the Apostles 1:7). Beyond that, however, this woman was being fundamentally ahistorical—a major problem when thinking about the new millennium.

The word "ahistorical," as it is applied here, means that the woman who scolded me wasn't placing current events in a broader (historical) context. She believed that she was experiencing things which had never before occurred in all the centuries in the history of the Church. This kind of ahistorical thinking often indicates that we've forgotten—or simply don't know—about similar incidents that happened in a period of history other than our own. When it comes to the history of apocalypticism, that old saying that there's nothing new under the sun has special meaning. Thinking historically helps us remember that fact.

Such self-centeredness with regard to the End is often found in history. Few people who predict the End say that they are *not* living in the final stages of the world. We all want to think that our era is the most exciting ever, but this desire can be another sign of our own self-centeredness and lack of humility. For our story, our human tendency toward self-centeredness is one more reason why apocalypticism offers a dangerous allure to a person seeking the meaning of his or her life. We all want to live in interesting times.

Living at the End would certainly be interesting, and the twentieth century may be the century of the world's largest technological advances and universal pain. But can it not be argued that the world was coming to an End for a peasant farmer in France in 1350 whose crops kept failing as the Black Death wiped out his village in a week? What about a young African taken away to slavery in the United States in 1790? Surely a Hebrew dragged from Jerusalem to Babylon in the sixth century B.C. could be forgiven for thinking that the End had come.

As far as these three extremely different people in widely-ranging circumstances were concerned, the world as they defined it was indeed ending. But this is just a piece of the picture. Only God sees the big picture—the whole picture—and he's not even telling his Son until it's time. Of course, the woman who accused me of being an academic who had "it all figured out" could easily be right: the End could occur right now, as you read this book. I simply wanted her to see that we can't count on that happening. There's no certainty, no proof, no way of figuring out definitively whether this is the century of the End or not.

Fortunately, a review of history can help us recognize past and current silliness, craziness, ignorance, and danger so that we can avoid mere repetition of the same, which will become increasingly popular in the media and maybe even in our own parishes. Avoiding such missteps may have been a primary goal for John Paul II who published his apostolic letter on the third millennium of Christianity in 1994, well in advance of growing interest in the End by the mass media, popular culture, and secular society. Before business executives and school superintendents drafted long-range plans to lead their companies and districts "into the twenty-first century," earlier than we elected a president for the "next millennium," sooner than television producers and Internet experts started airing prophecies which exploit people's fears, John Paul II laid down a plan for the Church. His letter, addressed not just to bishops and pastors but to all Catholics, was entitled *Tertio Millennio Adveniente* (*On the Coming Third Millennium*).

One of the most striking aspects of the letter is its historical approach. Several times, the Pope offers advice on moving forward into the third millennium that focuses on looking back at Church history, warts and all.

> Hence it is appropriate that, as the Second Millennium of Christianity draws to a close, the Church should become more fully conscious of the sinfulness of her children, recalling all those times in history when they departed from the spirit of Christ and his Gospel and, instead of offering to the world the witness of a life inspired by the values of faith, indulged in ways of thinking and acting which were truly forms of counter-witness and scandal (*Tertio Millennio Adveniente* #33).

Certainly the craziness of the past, in terms of apocalyptic expectations, is an example of counterwitness and scandal since many times, as we will see, some Christians saw themselves as a chosen elite. They took it upon themselves to judge others and call them forces of the Antichrist. These actions included labeling Muslims as the Antichrist's military troops and Jews as tools in the hands of the Antichrist. Within the Church herself, different groups fought for control by calling their fellow Catholics, including the pope, Antichrists.

Without understanding the terrible consequences of these past actions, we Catholics run the very plausible risk of repeating them in our current questions. One need only call to mind the fact that some Catholic writers who opposed Vatican II have used apocalyptic imagery to condemn the Council, noting that liturgical changes (such as turning the altar around and using vernacular language instead of Latin) or attitude shifts (like embracing the world) are evident signs that the forces of evil took over the Church during the meeting of the Second Vatican Council in the early 1960s.[2]

Talking About Terms

Before opening the history book of the Church to find more specific lessons, we must define our terms as best we can. Let's spend some time, then, talking about what we will talk about.

Historians do not agree on the definition of every term used in the discussion of the history of apocalypticism. Using the working definitions of scholars in history, sociology, and religion, however, we can generally define apocalypticism, eschatology, millenarianism, and millennialism.[3]

Apocalypticism is a prophetic sense that the End times are imminent. Apocalypticism is a more specific or definite treatment of the End than what is usually indicated by the word eschatology, which we will discuss next. The word apocalypse comes from the Greek word for revelation and means that a secret will be revealed. In the most familiar terms, this typically means that all of those seals and trumpets in the Book of Revelation tell a truth about the End which we can understand once someone like a prophet lets us in on the secret. That secret is some conception or timetable of world history which almost always includes the idea that we are living in the world's final stages. Therefore, apocalypticism is often linked to the effort to read the signs of the times to unveil the secrets which tell us how and when the End times will be played out.

Eschatology is a general notion that we are living in the last age of the world. This word, however, does not convey the immediacy or the particulars of the End as expressed by the word apocalypticism. In addition, eschatology is more frequently linked with the end of *our* individual lives or the physical End of the earth's life which will usher in *our* end. This is why most discussions of eschatology deal with personal salvation, heaven and hell, the resurrection of the dead, or meeting Saint Peter at the pearly gates.

Millenarianism and *millennialism* are closely related and often substituted one for the other. For the sake of uniformity and in light of the fact that this book does not seek to make fine academic distinctions, let's use only the word millenarianism and combine the common understanding of both terms.

Therefore, millenarianism is the belief that when the End comes according to Revelation 20:1-5, Christ (and, in some formulas, the saints) will rule on earth for one thousand years, a millennium (*mille* + *annus* in Latin), while Satan is locked up. This one-thousand-year reign will be one of peace and prosperity and will conclude with the Final Judgment and the End of the world. Some people, however, believe that this one thousand years of peace and prosperity will come *after* the End, but again we're not concerned with such debates here.

Two concepts are tied in with millenarianism. First, the word chiliasm, which comes from the Greek word meaning "one thousand," sometimes substitutes for millenarianism. Chiliasts are people who believe that the one-thousand-year reign is under way or on the way soon. They often identify themselves as good people living in the promised peace and prosperity or people who will usher in those good times. They often see the End in violent, destructive, and elitist terms. For these very reasons, both *Tertio Millennio Adveniente* (#23) and the *Catechism of the Catholic Church* (#676) specifically warn against such millenarian attitudes.

The second notion also connects with the one thousand years. If the world will have a millennium of prosperity while Christ reigns, then the Final Judgment will come at the end of that one thousand years. This is why some—but actually very few—people thought the world would end in 1000 or 1033, that is, one thousand years after Jesus was born, died, and rose from the dead. But since he didn't come in 1000 or 1033, he hasn't been reigning for one thousand years and so the year 2000 is meaningless.

And even if a thousand years was some kind of benchmark, the arithmetic doesn't work. Consider that most Scripture scholars and historians agree that Jesus was actually born between 6 and 4 B.C. That means that if one thousand (or, for some unknown reason, two thousand) years had to pass before Christ returns, then he would have come back in 994-996 (or 1994-1996). In other words, time passed and nothing happened.

The meaning of the millennium, then, clearly lies elsewhere. Following John Paul II's lead, let's look back before we move forward.

As we begin to review the history of apocalypticism, let me reassure you that history doesn't hurt. Even though there will be those dreaded names and dates that usually turn people off from history, please hang on because there is a greater and more important emphasis woven within the stories themselves. As we review the story of the Church, we will uncover specific lessons that a particular person, period, or movement holds for today's Church as we begin her third millennium of life.

Take particular note of the twin traditions of apocalypticism which emerge in the Early Church and continue through the centuries of history into our own day. The first tradition reflects destructive and panicked ways of looking for Jesus to return any minute, and interpreting current events as signs of the End. The second and preferred tradition reflects a constructive and personal method of being in a state of constant inner renewal so that whenever *the* End or *our* end comes, we'll be ready.

Notes

1. The following aspects of apocalyptic spirituality are drawn from Bernard McGinn, trans., *Apocalyptic Spirituality* (New York: Paulist Press, 1979), pp. 7-16, and *Antichrist: Two Thousand Years of the Human Fascination with Evil* (San Francisco: HarperSanFrancisco, 1994), pp. 10-16 and pp. 275-280.

2. McGinn, *Antichrist*, p. 252.

3. The following explanations are adapted from several sources, among them McGinn, *Visions of the End: Apocalyptic Traditions in the Middle Ages* (New York: Columbia University Press, 1979), pp. 1-14, and Dennis C. Duling, "BTB Readers Guide: Millennialism," *Biblical Theology Bulletin* 24 (Fall 1994): pp. 132-142.

Chapter One

Lessons from the Early Church

Christians have been looking for the End since the very beginning of the Church's history. The sense that Jesus would come again to judge the good and the evil, to separate the wheat from the chaff or the sheep from the goats as the gospels describe the Second Coming, was intense in the weeks following his Ascension into heaven forty days after rising from the dead. Because the idea that Jesus' return was still "any minute," some writers began to interpret the events of their day as signs of the End. But as more time passed and every prophecy or interpretation proved false—just like today's subway prophets who yell "The End is near!"—leaders of the Christian communities whom we call the Fathers of the Church urged an entirely different way of looking at the End. Stressing that Jesus said we don't know when the End will come, and that even he didn't know, the Fathers of the Church recommended that Christians stop waiting for the big End that wasn't coming (apocalypticism and millenarianism) and worry more about their own ends (eschatology). These Fathers introduced, then, an incredibly important idea: apocalyptic spirituality as a positive opportunity for personal reform. This is the most important lesson we can learn from the history of the Early Church.

Waiting for the Messiah to Come—or to Come Again?

The roots of apocalyptic expectations among the earliest Christians actually predate Jesus' birth. The Jews, you'll remember, had been waiting for the Messiah for many centuries. At the time of Jesus' birth, some Jewish leaders were particularly expecting that a political leader would come to deliver them from the authority of the Roman Empire which controlled Palestine. This is one reason why they did not recognize Jesus as the Christ, the Savior and Messiah. Expecting a political or military leader, they couldn't understand how this wandering, dusty carpenter with no apparent power could deliver them from Roman authority. To their eyes, Jesus was no king like David.

But that doesn't mean that the early Christians couldn't tap into their Jewish heritage for ideas about preparing for the Messiah. The difference, of course, is that the Jews who did not accept Jesus as the Messiah continued to await their Messiah. The new Christians, on the other hand, were waiting for Jesus to come *again*.

Specifically for our study of apocalypticism, the Jews had a long tradition of understanding persecution as an accepted part of their heritage; persecution would make them clean and ready for the Messiah to arrive—for the first time. This idea of purifying persecution, then, became enormously influential on the earliest Christian ideas of waiting for Jesus' *Second* Coming.

Let's turn to the Bible for clues as to how the first Christians picked up on Jewish ideas of the End to come. Certain key passages of what is now the Old Testament illustrate important Jewish ideas of suffering. Psalms 37, 49, and 73, along with Isaiah 24–27, take as their theme the question, "Why do the wicked prosper and the good suffer?" and tell of destruction and payment to come. The answer is that the wicked only *seem* to prosper and the good only *appear* to suffer because people are only thinking about what's happening on earth right now. These texts promised that there will be a reversal of fortunes at the End. The good will be rewarded in heaven and the wicked punished for their actions. This flip-flop of fates is clear also from Amos 5 and 9: those who suffer will enjoy a blessed life while those who cause suffering will experience eternal sorrow, just like the switch in fortune for the rich man and Lazarus in Jesus' well-known parable.

Let's draw two key ideas here. The first key idea comes from Psalm 37 which stresses that we must wait for the future: all of the verb tenses point ahead, not to the past or the present. "Will" and "shall" make us look forward with expectation. Isaiah 65 tells us *how* we are supposed to wait, which is the second key idea: the necessity of punishment for renewal in the new world that is to come. For there to be a blessed life, there must be a passage through sorrow and suffering. You can see how the early Christians who were being mocked, harassed, and persecuted for their belief in Jesus would seize on these ideas. Understanding that the pain of the present would lead to heavenly happiness in the future explained the need for the crucifixion to achieve the triumph of Easter and our salvation to come. This promised reward is why Saint Paul often encouraged his flock to glory in the cross.

A Bang or a Whisper:
How Will the Messiah Come–or Come Again?

The Jewish traditions of waiting for the End came into the Christian traditions not only through Paul, but through the Qumran community and John the Baptist, as well. The Qumran community was composed of a Jewish sect called Essenes who withdrew into the desert near Jerusalem about 170 B.C. until 68 A.D. and wrote what we now call the Dead Sea Scrolls. These scrolls speak of a time of hypocrisy to come and seven battles between good and evil. Each side will win three, and then God will come to help the good in the decisive seventh battle, sort of like the ultimate World Series clincher. They clearly expected the Messiah to come with a bang.

Here, again, is another piece of the Christian apocalyptic tradition, but one which will lead to trouble in the future—as we will see. The Qumran Essenes were "gnostic," which means that they believed the world held great truths and deep mysteries which they alone knew and had to guard. They were also dualists who thought everything could be separated into good and evil by following Deuteronomy 30:15: "See, I have set before you today life and prosperity, death and adversity." In their war scrolls, for instance, the Essenes at Qumran wrote of a Teacher of Righteousness and a Wicked Priest who led Sons of Light and Sons of Darkness against each other.

Life is always black and white like this for dualists. There is no room for a gray middle ground. Many times in history, a group would decide that it had the answer to the meaning of life or the secret that would unlock the Book of Revelation. Members of the group would withdraw to an isolated place—a desert, a military compound, a forest, or a hilltop—to arm themselves and await the End with violence. They would positively draw on Jewish and Christian traditions by stressing the need to persevere in goodness in the face of persecution by evil forces. But of course they would define themselves as the good and any opposition as evil. Sadly, this "us versus them" approach has always written a tragic chapter in the history of apocalypticism, one we'll see often as we turn the pages of the Church's family history photo album.

We mentioned earlier that John the Baptist was another means by which Jewish expectations for the Messiah were transmitted to the early Christian community. There is a lesson in John the Baptist's ideas of the End for us today. John the Baptist was probably looking for an apocalyptic figure that was fiery and powerful—someone to come with a bang. Recall that he shouted "Repent!" and therefore is a precursor of the emphasis on personal renewal and preparation for salvation that the Fathers of the Church and Pope John Paul II emphasize. But John the Baptist also seems to have expected Jesus to bring wrath and to lead a great battle on behalf of the kingdom of God.

John the Baptist must have been surprised at this quiet man of peace, love, and individual miracles. Maybe this is why he sent Jesus the question, "Are you the one or should we wait for another?" Jesus' answer is that the blind see, the lame walk, the dead rise, and the poor hear the good news (Matthew 11:2-6, Luke 7:18-23). In other words, Jesus says that, yes, he is the Messiah but that does not mean destruction and pain are imminent. Instead, Jesus offers health, life, and salvation—another important message that is often lost in all the smoke and mirrors.[1]

When Is Jesus Coming Back?

During the first one hundred and fifty years or so after Jesus died, Christianity spread throughout Asia Minor, Italy, and north Africa. But Christians didn't expect this world to last very long. Jesus told his followers that he would be with them always, even until the End of the world. Those followers heard "immediately—right away." Remember the scene from Ascension Thursday (Acts of the Apostles 1:6-12). Jesus' disciples, as Jews, asked him whether he was going to deliver them from the Romans by restoring the kingdom of Israel to the Jews. One wonders if Jesus was exasperated at the question! He replied by telling them—and us—that the time of the End was not for them to know. Jesus was then taken into the sky and disappeared behind a cloud.

And what did the disciples do? They stood there, as if they expected Jesus to pick up his keys and come right back down to usher in the End of the world, as he had just promised. The disciples stood there so long staring dumbfounded at the sky that two angels finally showed up, asked them what they were doing standing around looking up at the sky, and then sent them along their way. This belief in an immediate return is known as "imminence" because the disciples thought Jesus' return was imminent.

Although Jesus did not return that day or that weekend, the earliest Christians continued to believe that he'd be back any second. Because Jesus had gone with a promise to return, those left waiting had to prepare themselves. As a Jew, Saint Paul thought the End would be fiery, disastrous, and violent for those who were not deemed worthy by Jesus in his Second Coming. For all those who were worthy there would be eternal glory and salvation. Paul stressed a need for vigilance and for all to be in a state of constant readiness because the day of the Lord would come unexpectedly, like a thief in the night (1 Thessalonians 4:13-5:11).

Suffering in the "Last Days"

As we know, Jesus did not return right away. And while Christians waited for him, there were plenty of persecutions in those first few centuries under the Roman Empire. Christians saw this time as the "Last Days" before Jesus' return. Basing their idea of the End on the key themes of Jewish Scripture which we just reviewed, Christians saw their suffering as an essential characteristic of the End which they thought was going to occur any day.

The early Christians believed that their persecution was cleansing them and making them pure for the End—a belief firmly established in their Jewish heritage. Persecuted Christians, however, only *seemed* to suffer. Any pain was worldly pain and was nothing compared to the glory of the next world. This suffering began under the Roman emperors with Nero in 64 A.D. and continued sporadically between 193 and 305, especially under Emperors Decius and Valerian from 249 to 260. The Great Persecution under Diocletian (303-305) was the worst.

Throughout these persecutions, Christians used the ideas of Jewish Scripture and Paul's letters to encourage one another to remain strong and to accept their social and political oppression, their physical torture, even death. In that suffering they would imitate Christ and therefore participate in his Resurrection. The martyrs, especially, were examples to be copied. The stories of their courageous faith and their refusal to deny their Christian beliefs were passed around to encourage, inspire, and strengthen people as they continued to wait for Jesus to return—any minute.

An example of martyrdom will show how the earliest Christians saw their suffering as part of their eternal reward. In this selection from the *Martyrdom of Polycarp*, a bishop who died around the middle of the second century, martyrs are praised for suffering fire on earth so they would not have to suffer an eternal fire that would burn much hotter and longer.

Some of [the martyrs], so torn by scourging that the anatomy of their flesh was visible as far as the inner veins and arteries, endured with such patience that even the bystanders took pity and wept; others achieved such heroism that not one of them uttered a cry or a groan, thus showing all of us that at the very hour of their tortures the most noble martyrs of Christ were no longer in the flesh, but rather that the Lord stood by them and conversed with them. And giving themselves over to the grace of Christ they despised the tortures of this world, purchasing for themselves in the space of one hour the life eternal. To them the fire of their inhuman tortures was cold; for they set before their eyes escape from the fire that is ever-lasting and never quenched, while with the eyes of their heart they gazed upon the good things reserved for those that endure patiently....But they were shown to them by the Lord, for they were no longer men, but were already angels.[2]

The Dangers of a Persecution Complex

No one would deny the truth behind the statement that the life of the Early Church was watered by the blood of the martyrs. It's very important, though, to note a tendency among later groups to actually pursue martyrdom as a sign of their righteousness. Throughout Church history—and up to our own day, in fact—certain groups have claimed that their persecution by authorities, including Church authorities, proved they were right.

Although martyrdom as a witness to the faith of Christ grew from legitimate and praiseworthy roots, psychologists caution against this embrace of pain and suffering, especially when it is sought out rather than simply accepted. For example, the faithful witness of martyrs has often been abused in the history of apocalypticism by those eager to find a chance to battle for survival. Those looking for a fight will usually find one. From this position, it's not hard to move toward the desire to paint adversity—real or imagined—in terms of a great battle for glory. An apocalyptic, even paranoid, persecution complex is one negative development that grew from the positive example such as the martyrs' faith, courage, and hope.

Here, then, is a negative lesson. Members of many apocalyptic groups in the first couple of centuries of the Church's family history embraced the idea of a fiery End. Their beliefs gave meaning to their persecutions, to their lives and, ultimately, to their deaths. Like the Essenes of the Qumran community, they were gnostics who believed that certain special information had been revealed to them and to no one else. These gnostic or mystery cults seeking a fiery End held several notions that did not fit with Christianity and which were naturally inclined to that apocalyptic mentality where a group says that they ("us") have the truth behind special mysteries and no one else ("them") can gain it. Gnostics said that Church authorities could only understand part of the story of the End from Scripture. They, the gnostics, knew the whole story but couldn't share their secrets with the uninitiated.

The main problem with gnosticism as opposed to Christianity was the elite aspect. Gnostics said only they would be saved, which contradicted Jesus' statements that he had come for everyone. This sense of elitism often plays into an apocalyptic mentality. A member of any group or doomsday cult in our own time who claims to have the answer but will not share it, for instance, is really a modern-day disciple of this tradition of gnostic elitism.

Interpreting the Book of Revelation Word for Word

Finally, during the period of persecutions that was interpreted as the "Last Days," the idea of an imminent End was matched by a literal interpretation of prophecies in Scripture and popular culture. If Jesus was coming right away, then everything that was promised must be occurring. This led to a literal, what today is called fundamentalist, reading of Scripture. For example, Christians tried to see in Daniel, Revelation, the gospels, and other Scriptural texts clues that applied to their current circumstances. Most frequently, the

Roman Empire was identified with the Whore of the city of Babylon from Revelation 17 because the city of Rome had seven hills and ruled over all other kings just like Babylon in this passage. Many writers identified Rome as the earthly, immoral Babylon in contrast to the heavenly, spiritual Jerusalem over which Jesus will reign.

Specifically, Nero was identified as some apocalyptic figure, maybe even the Antichrist himself. Nero supposedly killed himself with his own sword but many mysteries surrounded his life and death. All of the rumors gave rise to the popular notion that he never really died; he received a fatal wound but magically it didn't actually kill him. Another idea was that he was dead but would rise again and return.

Some Christians linked Nero to Revelation 13:3 and 17:8, which refer to a wounded head of the beast from the sea. The wounded head lived, died, and would return after recovering from the wound. In the minds of some Christians, then, the stage was set for a Great Battle between Jesus, the champion of Good (Christ), and Nero, the champion of Evil (the Antichrist) that would occur any day.

This portrait of Nero's life increased both the literal interpretations of events and the urgent sense of the imminence of the End. But historical events soon made literalism and imminence less and less a possibility.

A More Personal Approach from the Fathers

So far, two factors have dominated the history of apocalypticism: a literal understanding of Scripture and a sense that the End was imminent. Both of these factors neatly fit into the Roman Empire. Rome was killing Christians so it must be evil according to the Christians being harassed, especially if the Romans were led by a tyrant like Nero or one of his persecuting successors. This notion that Rome was evil failed to work, however, when two events occurred that did not allow the anti-Roman brand of apocalypticism to succeed any longer. First, the Emperor Constantine converted to Christianity early in the fourth century. Constantine protected, then favored Christians. Rome could be the apocalyptic Babylon as long as Nero or other emperors persecuted the Church, but how could it be Babylon under a Christian emperor like Constantine? Second, after the Roman Empire began its long, slow crumble into nothingness in the fifth century, it couldn't play its new role as the champion of good versus a champion of evil. And after Rome fell, Jesus *still* hadn't come.

In short, imminence wasn't standing up over time and all literal interpretations were proving to be false. Rome fell—no End. As a result, much more fruitful, positive, and constructive ideas of the End had to emerge from the standard Jewish and early Christian elements of apocalypticism. They couldn't be dismissed, of course, since Jesus never denied that there would be an End.

The answer came from the Fathers who gave new explanations that were calmer than the imminent explanations and more rational than the literal interpretations. In a whole new way of thinking for Christian apocalypticism, the Fathers gave a spiritual interpretation of the End that tried to replace the literal reading of Scripture. Their spiritual interpretation did not focus so much on some huge portrait of the universal End where all of the current events around them fit into a big picture. Rather, they presented a much more intimate goal at which Paul had hinted: the constant readiness and persistent personal renewal of an individual soul preparing for his or her end. In so doing, they set the positive trends for apocalyptic spirituality that the Church has tried to follow since then. But these positive trends have often been obscured by the dangerous allure of the imminent-minded gnostics who claim to have the secrets behind the literal formulas.

Our Three Guides

Origen (ca. 185-254) was one of the first great Christian Scripture scholars, philosophers, and theologians. He was a brilliant thinker who could keep several secretaries busy by dictating multiple works at the same time. Origen spent most of his life in Alexandria and Palestine before dying in the persecution under the Emperor Decius. It is interesting to note that this is just the kind of persecution that led other writers to offer a literal understanding of the events of the day in their own times. But Origen went completely in the opposite direction.

Origen set himself very strongly against a literal reading of Scripture and the signs of the times to predict the End. Instead of focusing on the Antichrist figure, Origen asked people to consider the fact that evil can exist in any human heart. This is a much smaller concern, of course, than what filled the thoughts and actions of the chiliasts or millenarians who were competing with Origen for dominance in the field of Christian apocalyptic ideas. Anytime someone is a hypocrite or claims to have special information about God that he or she is not willing to share, Origen and the other Fathers taught, that person is acting like an antichrist. One scholar refers to this as an "interiorized reading" of Scriptural texts related to the End, especially 1 John 2:18-23 and 2 John 7 where the author of the letters warns that anyone who denies Christ is an antichrist.[3]

Does this mean that Origen and the Fathers said Christians should be running through the streets yelling "There's the Antichrist!" or that we should do the same today? Should we panic and look for signs of Satan inside each of us as if we were in one of those lousy Damien or *The Exorcist* movies? Absolutely not. To do so while mentioning Origen and the other Fathers would be an abuse of the Christian tradition.

Building on the author of John's letters, Origen told those of his own day (and we can say of ours as well) that we should be more concerned when we act against the way Jesus would have acted. Otherwise, we're bound to waste our time trying to interpret every action or event according to a mysterious book like Revelation, which is unclear anyway. And while we try to name the Antichrist, we'll miss opportunities to act like Christ.

Origen thought that interpretations based on current events served a limited purpose: to explain to simple minds how things *may* work out in the future. But he was much more concerned with how thinking about the End could improve people's spiritual lives in the most positive ways possible right here and now. In fact, he wrote, the End will only come fully when every human heart is made perfect.

Origen believed that the fulfillment of the world will take place step by step as each individual heart is perfected. "The kingdom of God will be fully established in us if we advance with ceaseless effort," Origen wrote in his treatise, *Prayer.* "Therefore, praying without ceasing with a disposition made divine by the Word, let us say to our Father in heaven: Hallowed be Thy name. Thy kingdom come."[4]

The next important person who moved away from literal, millenarian, and imminent ideas of the End was *Augustine* (354-430) who, like Origen, spent most of his life in north Africa. Augustine was a rising star in the secular world: a professor of rhetoric who spent his youth in a fairly wild and freewheeling life. After he experienced a torturous conversion—it took many years before he finally gave in to God—Augustine was ordained a priest and made bishop of a city named Hippo. The circumstances of his life, like those of Origen, strongly influenced his apocalyptic ideas.

As Augustine's life was coming to a close, the Roman Empire was in deep trouble. Barbarian tribes invading Europe chopped off large chunks of the Empire and the city of Rome itself was sacked. Because Rome was falling but the End was not arriving, Augustine saw that any literal interpretation was simply wrong. Think how easily, however, Augustine could have slipped into a panic. Not unlike that person who told me the twentieth century was the worst age ever, Augustine could have proclaimed that surely the signs of his times pointed to the End of the world.

However, in his famous work *City of God*, Augustine specifically mocked literal interpretations that fit the history of Rome's persecution of Christians into a scenario of the End based on the Book of Revelation. Step by step, he shot down prophecies by showing how they could be interpreted differently and remain just as "true" or "authoritative"—proving that such speculation was just as easily wrong as it was right. "I can see here no prophetic spirit but mere human guesswork which occasionally hits truth and just as often misses," he wrote. This reminds me of horoscopes or psychic friends' networks that are so vague they're bound to be on target some of the time because of the law of averages. Augustine went further:

> The more I ponder facts like these, the more I think we should abstain from trying to define the number of persecutions destined for the Church....So, I leave the question of future persecutions in a state of neutral indecision, neither building up nor tearing down either side, content to remind all to refrain from venturesome presumption....At this point people usually inquire: When will all this happen? A most unreasonable question, for, if it were good for us to know the answer, the Master, God Himself, would have told His disciples when they asked him (Acts 1:6-7)....Obviously, then, it is a waste of effort for us to attempt counting the precise number of years which this world has yet to go, since we know from the mouth of Truth [Jesus] that it is none of our business.[5]

Like Origen, Augustine saw that spending time figuring out the End based on current events was simply a waste of time. Such an effort did nothing but heap anxiety on people's minds. Therefore, Augustine set himself against millenarian, literal, and imminent ideas of the End and offered a more personal approach.

As bishop of Hippo, Augustine spent much of his time arguing against the Donatists and Pelagians, two groups of heretics who were very numerous and who had a strong sense of their own self-worth. As a young man, Augustine was attracted by another heretical group called the Manichees who saw the entire world in terms of forces of good and evil. Like those gnostics and dualists we've met before, the Manichees set themselves up as an elite that would be saved.

But rather than frightening the heretics around him into submission by telling them the End was coming, Augustine explained that they must make an account of their beliefs to God at their own ends. If a person accepted Christ, then the forces of evil were bound up and couldn't harm anyone. But if a person denied Christ, as noted in the letters of John, then evil was permitted into the world. Therefore, the job of the Christian, according to Augustine, is always to be on the lookout. Christians shouldn't let evil inside their hearts. Like Origen, Augustine emphasized a constant process of conversion in which people moved ever closer to God.

Finally, *Gregory I* (Pope from 590 to 604 and known as "the Great") saw Rome crumbling around him, only much worse than in the lifetime of Augustine. He himself actually had to sit down and convince an invading army to spare the city of Rome. To Gregory, objective evidence pointed to the final stages of a government and a society that had ruled the world for centuries. But Gregory persisted in using apocalyptic imagery to spur Christians to look within and to do so positively and with optimism. Even Gregory, however, could not fully escape the pessimism of his age. He seems to have believed that the End was on its way, though he didn't specify a day and date for the event. He spoke of a dying world, but instead of lamenting the fall of Rome, he saw it as a positive opportunity. Like Origen and Augustine, he saw a chance to boost spiritual reform in Christians' hearts. For Gregory, the End represented the chance to be saved regardless of when it arrived.

In his commentary on the Book of Ezekiel, Gregory asked a rhetorical question and then offered the answer. Listen closely to Gregory's words and hear echoes of the Jewish and early Christian understanding of the meaning of persecution.

> And why am I daily forced to drink bitter things when I can hasten to the sweet? What therefore remains except to give thanks with tears amidst the scourges we suffer for our sins?... Sometimes [the Father] nourishes his sons with bread, other times he corrects them with the scourge, since through sorrows and wounds and gifts he trains them for their eternal inheritance.[6]

If the End was on its way, as Gregory seemed to believe in general terms—as we do—then Christians were to seize the day to look within their own hearts, to repent, and to do good works on a spiritual level. Gregory encouraged Christians of his day to examine their lives, to reflect seriously and honestly on their spiritual states, and to persevere in their sufferings. The reward would come.

Notes

1. James D.G. Dunn, *Jesus and the Holy Spirit* (Philadelphia: The Westminster Press, 1975), pp. 55-60. I am grateful to Fr. Arthur Serratelli of Immaculate Conception Seminary at Seton Hall University for guiding me to this resource and discussing John the Baptist's expectations.

2. Cyril C. Richardson, trans. and ed., *Early Christian Fathers* (New York: Simon and Schuster, 1996), pp. 149-150.

3. Bernard McGinn, *Antichrist: Two Thousand Years of the Human Fascination with Evil* (San Francisco: HarperSanFrancisco, 1994), pp. 54-56 and pp. 64-65.

4. John J. O'Meara, trans., *Origen: Prayer. Exhortation to Martyrdom* (Westminster, MD: The Newman Press, 1954), p. 86.

5. Gerald G. Walsh and Daniel J. Honan, trans., *The Fathers of the Church*, vol. 24 (New York: The Fathers of the Church, Inc., 1954), pp. 174-177. These selections are from Augustine's *City of God*, book 18, chapters 52-53.

6. Carole Straw, *Gregory the Great: Perfection in Imperfection* (Berkeley: University of California Press, 1988), p. 184.

Chapter Two

Learning from the Middle Ages and the Reformations

Perhaps no periods in the history of apocalypticism are at the same time so colorful and so tragic as the Middle Ages and the Protestant and Catholic Reformations. For our purposes, we define that period broadly and roughly as 1000-1600 A.D. During these centuries, we'll see that the Fathers' emphasis on inner personal renewal was frequently lost—and small wonder. Amid all the noisy interpretations of certain contemporary events and rulers as the Antichrist or leaders against the Antichrist, who could look quietly within their own hearts?

Augustine had warned that literal interpretations were ultimately foolish and wrong. Fortunately, his stand against the idea of a one-thousand-year reign worked as a kind of official policy for Church leaders. But that didn't stop many Christians throughout the Church from continuing to be dazzled and fascinated by explanations of the signs of the times. Actually, some of these signs seemed to be true every now and again, at least a very little bit. But being true just a very little bit was enough for many, unfortunately.

Several trends surfaced in the history of apocalypticism during the Middle Ages. Probably more books and articles have been written about medieval and Reformation concepts of the End, especially as seen in art and literature, than about any other period. My purpose is not to review every single stage in that development; others have done that already and far better than I ever could. It's important, however, to step back from the details of these scholarly studies for two reasons.

First, turning a wide-angle lens on typical events or elements of any historical period is essential. Only when we pull back from the details can we distance ourselves from them to see the broader lessons which history teaches. Second, if we recounted all of the details here we would risk repeating what our medieval ancestors did: allowing ourselves to be distracted from the Fathers' personal message by flashy ideas of the End. So let's look at key snapshots from our Catholic family album to draw some lessons from Church history in the Middle Ages and Reformations.

Missing the Point

The positive aspects of apocalyptic spirituality will occasionally pop up as we continue listening to the family history of the Church. But all too often the negatives will be accentuated, to twist that old song around, and the positives will be eliminated. This tendency makes the Middle Ages and the Reformations probably the most distracting periods for positive apocalyptic spirituality and personal renewal. Too often, Christians in the Middle Ages and the Reformations just missed the point.

A story might help illustrate how this can happen. Not too long ago in the United States, a new Marine Corps general assumed a leadership role in Washington D.C. where military officers almost always wear their dress uniforms, polished shoes and buckles, and many medals and ribbons on their chests. This one particular Marine Corps general, however, never wore anything but his battlefield fatigues and always drank his coffee from a metal mess kit cup. He obviously didn't fit in with those around him, including his own staff. Asked by a reporter why he dressed and acted this way, the Marine Corps general grumbled, "Because we must always be prepared to go to war *tonight*."

Of course, I'm not telling this story to support those modern-day chiliasts who see every news event as a sign of Armageddon that justifies their stockpiling guns and hiding in a military compound. But this general had a point not unrelated to the Fathers' message. You never know when your end will take place, regardless of the End, so you must always be ready. That is a clear, crisp message that can easily be lost amid all the military spit and polish in Washington. That general did not let himself be distracted. He was not missing the point.

But in the Middle Ages and the Reformations people did miss the point. They let themselves be distracted from the Fathers' core message about constant, personal, inner spiritual renewal by flashy ideas of the End. One example may make my point. An abbot named Adso who lived in central Europe around 950 wrote an influential letter titled *Origin and Life of the Antichrist*. This letter summarized much of what people thought about the figure of the Antichrist in the legends which had developed from the first days of the Church until Adso's own lifetime.

Adso's account of the Antichrist, which was very popular in the Middle Ages, reads in places like a warped version of Christ's conception and birth as told in the New Testament.

> [Antichrist] will be born from the union of a mother and father, like other men, not, as some say, from a virgin alone. Still, he will be conceived wholly in sin, will be generated in sin, and will be born in sin. At the very beginning of his conception the devil will enter his mother's womb at the same moment. The devil's power will foster and protect him in his mother's womb and it will always be with him. Just as the Holy Spirit came into the mother of Our Lord Jesus Christ and overshadowed her with his power and filled her with divinity so that she conceived of the Holy Spirit and what was born of her was divine and holy, so too the devil will descend into the Antichrist's mother, will completely fill her, completely encompass her, completely master her, completely possess her within and without, so that with the devil's cooperation she will conceive through a man and what will be born from her will be totally wicked, totally evil, totally lost.[1]

When one of my students read this passage in a course I was

teaching, he described it as "icky." I agree. Who wouldn't be distracted from what really matters by this weird description? It triggers that natural human attraction for the bizarre. We may hate horror movies and car wrecks, but sometimes we have a morbid fascination with them. And when that fascination hits, we miss the point. This tendency, at bottom, is what we must learn from the history of apocalypticism in the Middle Ages and the Reformations.

Blaming Jews and Moslems: A Medieval Mob Mentality

The Middle Ages witnessed an upsurge in literal interpretations of current events in terms of the End—interpretations that often included Jews and Moslems. Some Catholics, for example, tried to fit certain events concerning Moslems into legendary and biblical prophecies, most often from the Book of Revelation. The advance of Islam appeared to fit into biblical prophecy because Islam did indeed threaten Europe on several occasions throughout the Middle Ages. Islam's founder Mohammed (ca. 570-632) and the famous Moslem military leader Saladin (1137-1193) were therefore depicted as the Antichrist's leaders rising from the eastern part of the world to challenge Catholic Europe. This interpretation was bolstered in 1187, when Saladin took Jerusalem back from the Christian Crusaders, and in 1453, when the Moslems gained control of Constantinople on the eastern side of Europe. Meanwhile, on the western side of Europe, Moslems held on to parts of Spain for many centuries until the Reconquest under King Ferdinand and Queen Isabella was completed in 1492. Until then, some Catholics felt hemmed in on both sides by the Moslems.

Jews were also frequently seen as a necessary evil. In many versions of the End times, Jews, thinking that the Antichrist was the Messiah, would follow him to Jerusalem and resettle in the Promised Land. In other legendary versions of the End, Moslems and Jews would be converted in massive numbers. When the traveling Dominican Vincent Ferrer (ca. 1350-1419) converted many Moslems and Jews across Europe with his preaching, some saw this as a sure sign that the End was coming, a fact that may have been promoted by Vincent's own statements that the Antichrist had been born in his lifetime.

What happened around 1009 was far more troubling than these legends and mass conversions. In that year, a Moslem leader ordered that Jerusalem's Church of the Holy Sepulchre, the site of Jesus' burial and resurrection, be burned to the ground. As a result, the leader, a caliph named Hakim, was identified as the Antichrist by Christians because of his desecration of this holiest Christian place. In France, some Christians added rumors to the event, claiming that the Jews had pushed Hakim to destroy the Church of the Holy Sepulchre. In response, Christians took revenge by baptizing many Jews against their wills and even murdering others.[2]

Looking back at this scene that was so tragic for three religions, we can ask how such actions were in line with Augustine's cautions against literal interpretations of events. Even more harshly, we can wonder how killing Jews or forcing them to convert to Christianity was a way of following the Fathers' message of inner personal renewal.

Beware the Antichrist!

Another major trend in the Middle Ages was the identification of certain religious and political leaders as the Antichrist. It is shocking to read how far even popes and emperors would go to label their enemies as the Antichrist. They painted any opposition to themselves and the Church or the Empire in demonic, apocalyptic terms.

When Frederick II (Holy Roman Emperor, 1215-1250), for example, fought the papacy and criticized the worldliness of the Church, Gregory IX (Pope, 1227-1241) excommunicated the emperor and referred to him as the beast from the sea (Revelation 13:1-2). Just a few weeks later, which was very quickly in medieval terms, Frederick II fired a similar accusation right back at the Pope:

The Roman pontiff of our time, a Pharisee sitting in the seat of false doctrine and anointed with the oil of evil beyond all his fellows, has stopped following the heavenly order and strives to abolish all this....He, who is pope in name alone, has said that we are the beast rising from the sea full of the names of blasphemy and spotted like a leopard....[H]e is that great dragon who leads the world astray (Revelation 12), Antichrist, whose forerunner he says we are.[3]

Gregory IX responded by linking the emperor with the Antichrist and the Moslems:

What other Antichrist should we await, when, as is evident in his works, he is already come in the person of Frederick? He is the author of every crime, stained by every cruelty, and he has invaded the patrimony of Christ, seeking to destroy it with Saracen aid.[4]

The battle even went beyond the grave. When Frederick unexpectedly died, his enemies claimed he hadn't really died and would return just like another Nero.

Here, then, is a perfect example of world leaders acting like children trying to top each other in a backyard squabble. The abuse of the New Testament discussions of the End is clear, while the Fathers' message of personal renewal is completely lost. But think of the headlines this rhetoric would have drawn if CNN and tabloid newspapers had been around in 1239!

Some Misconceptions: What People *Didn't* Do in the Middle Ages

Our perceptions of how the End was anticipated in the Middle Ages are actually poorly informed. For example, it was long believed that the Year 1000 was full of doom and gloom, with most people expecting the End any second. This picture, however, does not stand up to historical evidence. The fact is, very few people beyond an elite of trained clerics thought about the End. We must remember that the Year 1000 didn't see desk calendars and date books in the hands of every person in the world. As one scholar pointed out, did the medieval equivalent of the person in the street even *know* it was the Year 1000? Probably not.

Another misconception that persists is that the Black Death led to another huge outbreak of apocalyptic hysteria. The Black Death, now known to have been the bubonic plague, swept through the Mediterranean world and Europe from the Far East in the middle of the 1300s and kept returning for several centuries. While some people became fascinated with death in their spirituality, art, literature, and popular songs and rituals during this period, others tried to date the End. But, again, there seems to have been concern only among a very small minority of educated scholars that this event was connected with the End in a clear and undeniable way.

The Year 1000—which at least had some vague meaning for literal millenarians and chiliasts fascinated by the idea of a spectacular thousand years—did not usher in the End or even lead to widespread concerns. Why, then, should the Year 2000 lead to greater apocalyptic concerns when it has absolutely no mathematical meaning for the End? Likewise, since the Black Death wasn't the End, why should people point with great certainty to AIDS as a sign of the End, as some are doing?

Misconceptions of history's events such as those we've just recounted ought to be remembered as we experience the Year 2000 and beyond. If Christians today hold on to believing in these two misconceptions that have been proven false, then they risk repeating mistakes of the past which never even actually happened.

The Good, the Bad, and the Ugly

A medieval element of the End which was, by contrast, very influential was the idea that the world was getting older and moving closer to God. The most important thinker for this aspect of apocalypticism in the Middle Ages—maybe the most important thinker for any aspect of apocalypticism in any era for that matter—was Joachim of Fiore (1135-1202). What we find in the writings of Joachim and in the actions of those who used and misused his ideas are many of the positive and the negative aspects of apocalyptic spirituality: the good, the bad, and the ugly. From this part of our Church's family history, then, we can learn both what we should do and what we should avoid as we move into the Church's third millennium.

Joachim was an abbot who wrote many things about the End. He saw the world as having three stages. According to Joachim, each stage overlaps the next stage and the end of one is accompanied by confusion or some outbreak of evil. Each stage is announced in the previous stage by a prophet. Joachim's approach was literal. He and his followers used his writings to interpret current events in terms of the End. For example, he believed that Sacred Scripture prophesied the rise and fall of historical figures we've already seen related to the End, including Nero, Mohammed, and Saladin.

Unfortunately, it's easy to get lost when reading Joachim. He seems contradictory in places because of the overlapping stages of the world's lifetime. What's more, some of what Joachim discussed was snatched up by people who abused his ideas—ideas that were actually very traditional in their cores and followed the Fathers' concern with individual growth. His literal interpretations of Scripture, however, clearly did not follow the Fathers' advice, especially Augustine's warnings. These interpretations, because they were enticing and fascinating, overshadowed his message of inner renewal.

For instance, Joachim wrote that a future holy pope would be aided by spiritual men and that the End would be accompanied by the conversion of the Jews. After Joachim's death, some groups identified themselves as those spiritual men. These men acted very much like the gnostic elites of early Christianity who said they had all the answers and the purity, and that their enemies would burn in hell. Such groups saw in their own persecution proof that they were indeed the chosen few and reveled in the traditional apocalyptic mentality in which the End gave meaning to one's life.

Why is the reemergence of gnostics in the Middle Ages important for us today? Precisely because the patterns they followed can easily come up again in our own world, as we will see soon enough. For now, we should pay attention to the models of the Spiritual Franciscans and the Taborites which later groups often imitated.

One of these medieval groups of the "self-appointed pure" was the Spirituals. They were a group of Franciscans who became convinced that the Antichrist had taken over the papacy itself. This fact was "proven," according to the Spirituals, when several popes began to condemn the group's insistence on the absolute poverty of Jesus and of their own religious community. As a result, the Spirituals believed that the pope himself was the Antichrist. That charge is shocking enough when it comes from an emperor fighting a pope. But it's even more shocking when it comes from within the Church herself.

Another elitist and chiliastic group in the Middle Ages was the Taborites. They were political, social, and religious revolutionaries who saw themselves as an elite in eastern Europe. The Taborites believed that Jesus would come again in February 1420 so they sold their houses and property. With a military mentality and plenty of military equipment they then withdrew into isolated, armed communities in the hills around Prague and other Czech cities. As the elect, the Taborites felt they had a duty to rob and even kill the nonelect in the cities below them. When Jesus did not arrive in February 1420 as they had expected, however, the Taborites took it upon themselves to punish "the unworthy."

Clearly, then, the bad and the ugly that grew out of Joachim of Fiore's writings overshadowed the good. The Taborites were clearly far from Joachim's idea of the spiritual men. Obviously, what was lost in some of the imaginative thoughts of Joachim were the Fathers' teachings on personal renewal. For example, Joachim believed that with each stage the world and the humans in the world were getting closer to God. He was spelling out a kind of spiritual journey in which people grew closer to God by wrestling daily with Scripture, by studying and meditating over Scripture, and by praying for enlightenment and understanding from God.

These were mainstream aspects of medieval piety which focused on very personal devotions and a person's individual relationship with God. They are among the good characteristics that appear to be resurfacing in our own times as people search for a close connection with the Lord. But these characteristics are also threatened by the bad and the ugly medieval traditions. It's important, then, to learn from the good lessons and to avoid the mistakes of our medieval Christian brothers and sisters.

Shining a Light in the Darkness

The Middle Ages culminated in some of the darkest, most troubled decades in the family history of the Church. During the Avignon Papacy (1305-1378), the popes and cardinals set up a permanent administration in southern France, far from the papacy's traditional home in Rome. The Great Western Schism (1378-1417) saw two, and then three, rival popes claim to be the true and legitimate successor to the chair of Saint Peter.

The Avignon Papacy and the Great Western Schism had obvious applications to those interested in seeing the Antichrist emerge from within the Church herself. If there were several popes and lots of corruption in Avignon, some argued, at least one of the popes and colleges of cardinals had to be evil. The Italian poet Petrarch (1304-1374), for instance, saw the tremendous financial and ethical corruption of the Avignon curia as proof that the Whore of Babylon had taken over the papal administration.

It is interesting to note, however, that the Schism was *not* the occasion of massive apocalyptic propaganda. Here is light in the darkness. True, some people naturally labeled one pope or the other as the Antichrist. But writers and preachers were not so much interested in giving a line-by-line, literal interpretation of the Book of Revelation as stating that the Antichrist could infect the hearts of confused Christians and take over the disunited Church. In fact, many in the Church at that time taught us a very important lesson for today: the darkest, most difficult times do not necessarily translate into moments when delirium, hysteria, and panic have to take over.

In the life of the Church, as in our individual and family lives, we sometimes learn more from the tough times than the happy. Consider this. Augustine had good reason to think that the fall of Rome was the end of at least an era. But he did not become a prophet of doom and gloom by literally translating the events of his lifetime as heralds of the End according to the Book of Revelation. So, too, during Avignon and the Great Schism; many people took the situation as an opportunity to call for reform instead of ruin. In this way, the Schism was actually a moment when the Fathers' emphasis on reform reemerged amid some flamboyant, literal ideas of the End and the righteous claims of gnostic elites like the Taborites.

Writing about a period of Church reform in the eleventh and twelfth centuries, the historian Bernard McGinn states that "people who used apocalyptic imagery both expected the end and used end-time symbols for their own present purposes. The process of understanding present conflicts in terms of symbols of the End can have apocalyptic significance even in the absence of definite prediction about the imminence of the last things."[5] Many faithful Christians in the fourteenth and fifteenth centuries also used apocalyptic imagery to issue a call for reform without themselves being absolutely convinced that the End was literal and imminent.

Among those prophetically calling for reform during the Avignon Papacy was Bridget of Sweden (ca. 1302-1372). Bridget said she was sent by Christ to call for the papacy's moral and financial reform as well as its return to Rome. Note that she was not calling for the end of the papacy or the overthrow of the Church.

There was no need to panic, but it was necessary for Christians to change and to grow. One Christian who wrote in this way was a professor at the University of Paris who spent some time in Avignon: Nicolas de Clamanges (ca. 1363-1437). Clamanges' good friend Jean Gerson, who was working to resolve the Great Schism, once said that the Church had lost her way at this time. Reformers like Clamanges and Bridget were trying to help the Church find her way back. They used evocative apocalyptic images to capture people's attention so they wouldn't miss the larger point made by the Fathers. Personal reform would serve them well if the End came tomorrow or a million tomorrows later.

Clamanges often turned to Scripture to make his point about the need for personal renewal in the face of impending judgment. In a treatise titled *On the Ruin and Renewal of the Church*, Clamanges reminded his readers of the destruction of Sodom and Gomorrah (Genesis 18:16-19:29). However, Clamanges also noted that God had investigated the cities before destroying them. In making that point, he intended to tell his readers that they still had a chance to appease an angry God. He also used the story of the evil twin sisters Oholah and Oholibah (Ezekiel 23) with the Whore of Babylon (Revelation 17-18). The sisters were prostitutes in Egypt who represented the lack of faith of the Hebrews. Oholah and Oholibah were very promiscuous. Their sins finally piled up against them and they were repaid with destruction. This is exactly what will happen to the Whore of Babylon as well, he wrote in another treatise which criticized priests and bishops who bought and sold their parishes and dioceses.

Clamanges also used Jesus' familiar parable of the weeds and the wheat (Matthew 13:24-30,36-43) to remind his readers of the need for personal reform so they would be ready to be judged by God whenever that time came. As we know, the parable tells of an enemy who sowed weeds among the wheat planted by a farmer. When both the wheat and the weeds grew side by side, the farmer was asked whether the weeds should be pulled out. The farmer responded that at harvest time both the wheat and the weeds would be collected together. They would then be separated, with the wheat going into storage and the weeds being burned. In explaining the parable, Jesus noted that the harvest represented the End when the faithful would be judged worthy of heaven or hell. Clamanges' point in using this parable was to remind Christians that whether we die at the End or our own end, we must be ready to be judged.

A great but overlooked lesson from the apocalyptic imagery used during the Avignon Papacy and the Great Schism, therefore, is that people were honestly and justifiably pessimistic about the present. They had no illusions that a divided Christendom was nothing to be proud of. But they were optimistic that the situation could be resolved and that better times would come soon if they worked from within themselves and within the Church for reform. And if only from the standpoint of the papacy, their times were surely much worse than our own. They had three popes and confusion, after all, while there's no argument as to who our pope is right now.

Prophets of Doom

To be fair, positive aspects of apocalyptic spirituality were not the only characteristics of medieval apocalypticism; prophets of doom were not entirely out of the picture. As we noted the Taborites sought an overthrow of Church and civil government rather than constructive reform. Other critics continued to use Antichrist language to attack the Church in a foreshadowing of the Protestant Reformation and Martin Luther's identification of the papacy with the Whore of Babylon. It is important to note, as McGinn reminds us, that long before Luther, medieval Catholics themselves—like the Spiritual Franciscans and Emperor Frederick II—wielded the Antichrist as a weapon.

We can say, then, that at the close of the Middle Ages, Catholics had learned very little from the lessons of Church history. A fair number of preachers, for example, were still claiming to read the signs of the times in terms of literal interpretations of the End. There were so many, indeed, that the Fifth Lateran Council had to legislate in its 1516 decrees that no cleric should preach that he knows the time of the Antichrist's coming and the date of the End.

Nor shall [preachers] presume to announce or predict in their sermons any fixed time of future evils, the coming of Antichrist or the day of the Last Judgment, since the truth [Jesus] says: "It is not for you to know the times and moments which the Father hath put in his own power" (Acts of the Apostles 1:7). Those who till now have made such and similar predictions have lied, and their conduct has been in no small measure a detriment to the esteem and work of those who preach well. Wherefore, no cleric, whether regular or secular, who engages in this work in the future is permitted in his sermons to foretell future events [from Sacred Scripture] or to affirm that he has received his knowledge of them from the Holy Ghost or through divine revelation or to resort for proof of his statements to foolish divinations....[6]

On the eve of the Reformations, the pope and bishops had to scold their own preachers who claimed to be self-appointed prophets with divine revelations. They had to remind those preachers that it's not for us to know when the End will occur. Before we modern-day Catholics accuse Protestants of a history of dangerous and divisive tactics, therefore, we should look first to our own medieval history. If medieval Catholics didn't learn the lessons of Church history, at least we can learn from their mistakes today.

Beware the Antichrist! The Reformation Sequel

The age of the Protestant and the Catholic Reformations is perhaps the worst example of the "us versus them" mentality in which one group stains the other with apocalyptic accusations. It's as if people are literally saying "Go to hell!" to their opponents. This tradition, though sad, is an important one to remember, especially in today's Vatican II Church which calls us to bring Christian churches together instead of acting in a way that pushes us all further apart. And conveniently forgetting the tradition of Protestant-Catholic animosity because it's distasteful is like sweeping dust under the rug. It's still there and piling up. Better to face the bad and ugly parts of our tradition so we don't repeat them. We'll begin with the Protestant Reformation.

The identification of the papacy and curia with the Antichrist and his helpers was central to Protestant criticisms of the Catholic Church during the 1500s. But two facts must be kept firmly in mind. First, the Catholic Church was indeed in great need of reform in the late Middle Ages. Research emerging in the last thirty years points to Catholic efforts at reform before the Protestant Reformation. This tells us that Catholics were well aware of their faults before Martin Luther, but they were largely unsuccessful in doing anything about them. Second, as we have already seen, the Protestants were not the first to use Antichrist and apocalyptic images toward the papacy. In that sense, they were simply continuing and applying a sad chapter in Catholic history in a more forceful way.

The most famous step in this process of extending apocalyptic imagery was Martin Luther's statement in *The Babylonian Captivity of the Church* (1520): "The papacy is indeed nothing but the kingdom of Babylon and of the true Antichrist." His 1535 translation of the Bible into German identified the Whore of Babylon (Revelation 17-18) with the papacy. In 1545, a ridiculous extreme was reached when an illustration in *The Depiction of the Papacy* portrayed the devil defecating the pope and his cardinals.[7]

Luther's criticisms and apocalyptic imagery were quickly radicalized by his followers across Europe. Some took up where the Taborites left off, linking religious criticism with social and political upheavals. Thomas Müntzer, a radical follower of Luther, saw the entire social system of Germany in the early sixteenth century as part of the Antichrist's plan to destroy the world. He led an elect to bring about the Second Coming and thereby counterattack the Antichrist. Müntzer, reviving chiliasm, believed that armed conflict would lead to one thousand years of peace and prosperity on earth after the papal Antichrist had been defeated. Müntzer's elitism and embrace of persecution were mirrored in France, though less violently. During the next century, French Protestants known as

Huguenots were led by Pierre Jurieu who interpreted the Catholic King Louis XIV's persecution of them as evidence that the End was near. Their suffering proved to them that they were the spiritual elite who had to keep the faith like the martyrs of the early Church.

Protestants Versus Catholics: Name-Calling in the Schoolyard

Pretty soon, as McGinn observes, the Antichrist was everywhere! Ironically, even some of Luther's followers went so far in their eagerness to root out the Antichrist that they began to see the Antichrist among the Protestants themselves, just as some Catholics saw the Antichrist in the papacy. Anyone who sought compromise between Catholics and Protestants was labeled a traitor and the Antichrist.

In England, some thought the Anglican Church founded by King Henry VIII was still too Catholic. These people called themselves Puritans, for their purity to the Protestant Reformation, and labeled both Roman Catholic and Anglican bishops as agents of the Antichrist. The sublime turned ridiculous a century later when one English writer took the trouble to calculate that "666" was the pope's street address in Rome.[8]

Once more, then, we see small groups of people like the Puritans fascinated by the End. Its members identified themselves with the spiritual elite who would endure suffering and be declared worthy at the End. At the same time, they usually identified the Antichrist among their enemies. Such an effort, as always, simply distracted people from looking for sin within their own hearts.

The Catholics, however, don't come out of this story wrapped in innocence. They were just as guilty as the Protestants of pointing the Antichrist finger. Catholics countered Luther's charges against the papacy, for example, with their own literal interpretations that Luther was the Antichrist or somehow related to him. According to one interpretation, Lutherans were the locusts in the

Book of Revelation, and Luther himself was the star falling from heaven and the beast from the land.

In an even more direct counterattack to Luther's identification of the papacy with the Antichrist, the Jesuit Robert Bellarmine wrote a series titled *Disputations Concerning the Controversies of the Christian Faith Against the Heretics of This Time* (1586-1593). In the third part, "On the Antichrist, Who Has Nothing in Common with the Roman Pontiff," he debunked Luther's claims that the papacy was the Antichrist in the present time. He argued back that the Antichrist would be one person who would appear at some point in the future.

But Bellarmine did not stop with a simple defense of Catholicism. He himself went on the attack by arguing that the name Martin Luther could be seen as the "666" sign of the Antichrist. Returning to earlier traditions that had been lost in the identification of the pope or emperor as the Antichrist, Bellarmine argued that the Antichrist would be a Jew.

Meanwhile, other Catholics exploited certain inconsistencies, ambiguities, and open questions in Protestant discussions of the Antichrist and the papacy. Catholics tried to beat Protestants at their own game. Some argued the prophecies of the Book of Revelation in literal terms. One Jesuit identified certain scenes from Revelation with the Roman emperor Constantine and the fall of the Roman Empire. A French Catholic bishop saw one verse fulfilled by the invasions of Attila the Hun.

But these Catholic writers were flawed because they were trying to play both sides of the court. They claimed on the one hand that some of Revelation's prophecies could be identified with past events. On the other hand, they denied that other current events could fit into apocalyptic scenarios or that future apocalyptic events could be predicted with certainty.

Clearly, then, it was easy for Reformation Catholics defending their faith and pope to get sucked into the interpretation game. The same holds true today. When we try to refute certain prophecies, we usually end up arguing on our opponents' turf by using their literal examples. It can be argued, for example, that the Jesuits had no choice but to try to match the Protestants. Nevertheless they were distracting themselves and others from Augustine's advice that calculating the End is a waste of time and that Christians ought to concentrate on personal renewal instead.

It doesn't take great historical insight to recognize a basic and sad fact. Even more so than in the Middle Ages, the Reformations saw Catholic and Protestant Christians allowing themselves to be distracted from the core ideas of the Fathers about personal renewal. They were too busy occupying themselves with charges, defenses, and countercharges concerning the Antichrist. There was little concern with apocalypticism, which at least can be praised if it is constructively focused on preparing for the End, and none at all for eschatology, which focuses the Christian on his or her personal end.

Since most efforts were spent on labeling others with the taint of the Antichrist, we might wonder how much time, if any, was spent on looking within. This may be the most important lesson that the Middle Ages' literalism and the Reformations' obsessive fascination with the figure of the Antichrist have for Christians in the third millennium.

Notes

1. Bernard McGinn, trans., *Apocalyptic Spirituality* (New York: Paulist Press, 1979), pp. 90-91.
2. Jonathan Sumption, *Pilgrimage: An Image of Medieval Religion* (Totowa, NJ: Rowman and Littlefield, 1975), p. 133.
3. McGinn, *Visions of the End: Apocalyptic Traditions in the Middle Ages* (New York: Columbia University Press, 1979), pp. 174-175.
4. McGinn, *Antichrist: Two Thousand Years of the Human Fascination with Evil* (San Francisco: HarperSanFrancisco, 1994), pp. 153-154.
5. McGinn, *Antichrist*, p. 120.
6. H.J. Schroeder, trans., *Disciplinary Decrees of the General Councils* (London: Herder, 1937), p. 505.
7. McGinn, *Antichrist*, pp. 201-210.
8. Richard Popkin, "Seventeenth-Century Millenarianism," in *Apocalypse Theory and the Ends of the World*, ed. Malcolm Bull (Oxford: Basil Blackwell, 1995), p. 113.

Chapter Three

America: A New Beginning for the End

Something strange happened to the place of Christian faith in society as the world became more "modern," starting with the Scientific Revolution and the Enlightenment of the 1600s and 1700s. Christianity, the center of everyone's existence and the organizing glue of society in Europe for almost fifteen hundred years, began to lose out to a whole new batch of modern ideas that were sometimes grouped together as the "isms." These "isms" were intellectual, political, social, and economic movements that dominated European, and then American, society in the modern era. In politics, constitutionalism and nationalism pushed the American revolutionaries to establish a democracy free from the British government. Nationalism became a rabid, almost fanatical love of country that sometimes put a person's first loyalty not to God but to nation. Rationalism and secularism also pushed religion into the background. In the worst cases, faith in God was laughed at. Only stupid, ignorant, or superstitious people would continue to believe in God. Science, after all, was proving that other forces— like chemistry and biology—were really running the human body, the weather, and the planets. The poet Alexander Pope, noting the significance of Isaac Newton's study of physics, even flipped the Book of Genesis around to read, "God said, 'Let Newton be' and all was light."[1]

America: Apocalyptic Religion in Her Blood

Now, not all of the extreme rationalism and secularism from the Scientific Revolution and the Enlightenment crossed the Atlantic Ocean with the Pilgrims on the Mayflower. What happened was that the first immigrants brought their religious traditions with them and then married those traditions with their modern nationalistic pride in America. The result, as we will see, was a melting pot full of political, religious, and social apocalyptic ideas.

Since the story of the apocalyptic movement in America is more instructive for the Church today as she enters the third millennium, we now turn to the history of apocalypticism in our own country. The religious roots of American apocalypticism can be traced all the way back to the early Church through the Middle Ages and the Reformations. We may not realize it, but Christian apocalypticism is part of the blood and bones of the vision of America as a great nation. Despite our secular society, Christian apocalypticism is alive—and both well and dangerous—in our own day. It has much to teach us today in the United States.

Nationalism in America had strong religious—especially apocalyptic—overtones and has almost become a civic religion in itself. Unfortunately, those apocalyptic overtones have often been the negative, destructive, literal types that try to read the signs of the times and lead to resurgences in elitism, gnosticism, and a panicked fear that "The End is near!" Every time people yell, "America, love it or leave it!" they exclude a portion of the population—and that is not what Jesus' message of salvation is all about.

Just as it is impossible to understand the first moments of Christian apocalypticism without understanding the Jewish world into which Jesus was born, it is impossible to understand American apocalypticism without realizing that America is a country with religion in her blood. In fact, the very first book published in America was a version of the Psalms. If people owned one book, it was the Bible. And a poem with huge popularity among the first settlers dealt with the Last Judgment with the ominous title, "The Day of Doom."

Simply consider all of the rhetoric that accompanies politics and government in the United States, starting with the language of the preamble to our Constitution:

We the People of the United States, in order to form a more perfect Union, establish justice, insure domestic tranquility, provide for the common defense, promote the general welfare, and secure the blessings of liberty to ourselves and our posterity, do ordain and establish this Constitution for the United States of America.

Many of those words reach toward an ideal society in the future that recall earlier chiliast views of heaven on earth: a more perfect union, general welfare, the blessings of liberty for ourselves and our posterity, a plan that is ordained. That is not to say that the fathers who framed the Constitution in Philadelphia in 1787 were apocalypticists, only that America's traditions of Enlightenment optimism and religious imagery ran deeply in their veins.

Long before the American Revolution and the Constitutional Convention, America had religious roots connected with apocalypticism, the End, and a millennium of peace and prosperity. One scholar of American literature put it nicely.

Images of the end of the world abound in American literature, and with good reason: the very idea of America in history *is* apocalyptic....Discovered by Europeans in the sixteenth century, America was conceived as mankind's last great hope, the Western site of the millennium. Settled by millenarian religious groups, most notably the Puritans in the Massachusetts Bay Colony, its future destiny was firmly and prophetically linked with God's plan for the world, and the national dream of an American Age, a great paradisal future to be ushered in by America, remains strong even in our own time.[2]

As this scholar pointed out, that story starts with those Plymouth Rock settlers from the Mayflower. We usually recall them as the "Pilgrims," but they considered themselves the "Puritans"—purer than other Protestant Reformers in England in the 1600s.

Listen again to that familiar story of the Mayflower Pilgrims—but this time with an ear tuned to the apocalyptic dimensions, maybe for the first time. You'll hear overtones of the history of apocalypticism that we've been exploring so far. Those overtones will help us understand the heritage of apocalypticism that falls to Americans in the late twentieth century.

The Puritans were religious people who fled persecution to achieve religious freedom. As a small band of outcasts, they kept to themselves and deliberately separated themselves from others by a wide ocean as they sought freedom of worship. In the Mayflower Compact (1620), the Puritans stated "solemnly and mutually in the presence of God" that they had taken their dangerous journey across the Atlantic in part "for the glory of God, and advancement of the Christian faith."

For these Puritans, America was the land of opportunity, the shining city on a hill, a "New World." But it was also an unknown, harsh, and uncompromising forest. Like a lost tribe of Israel searching for the Promised Land, they wandered through that forest and underwent purifying trials as they persevered.

You can see, then, that from the time the first settlers came ashore, America saw herself as a divinely-chosen spot on earth. This identification of America as a "promised land" and Americans as a chosen people fits neatly with the apocalyptic idea that God will choose a certain group of people in a special place and let them flourish at the End of time. The fact that life in America was very difficult, especially as settlers struggled through their first few winters in what became Massachusetts and Virginia, only increased the parallels between Americans as elect and the apocalyptic scenario of cleansing fires that made people pure and worthy of the Last Judgment.

Polishing the Shining City on a Hill

America's sense that she was predestined for greatness continued to intersect with apocalypticism throughout her history. It becomes even more pronounced whenever anyone puts a date on the End of the world by interpreting events in American life, politics, or culture as signs of the End.

Moving from the first generations of settlers into the eighteenth century, however, the optimistic side of apocalyptic hope came to be painted in darker terms. What we begin to hear more frequently is a call to reform not unlike that of the Fathers of the Church, but one that was usually heard as a parent scolds a disobedient child. The extremism which overlooks the positive aspects of the Fathers' call for personal renewal and is such a danger today, therefore, also has its roots in the earliest stages of America's story as a nation.

The purity of those first Pilgrims declined in the century after the Mayflower landed. As Americans settled farther away from the coast into New England, they grew rich, fat, and lazy. As with our own age, materialism became a very attractive, alluring, and distracting alternative to religion. As the pews began to empty, preachers tried to frighten their congregations to return to God.

In response to this creeping materialism, the rigorous Puritan preacher Jonathan Edwards (1703-1758) started a "Great Awakening" of Puritan life and aimed to scare his parishioners straight through a literal interpretation of the Book of Revelation. Edwards resurrected many of the old legends of the End: the conversion of the Jews, the onslaught of the Moslems, the martyrdom of the good in a Great Battle. Although Edwards preached that the End was very near, he didn't set a date; he simply urged his flock to be at the front of the line in returning to God.

Edwards told his congregation that they were all sinners in the hands of an angry God; that nothing stood between them and the fires of hell but the thinnest strand of a thread; that if they didn't stop sinning they'd burn in hell. As a result, many people got swept up with emotion and began to fear for their lives. Because their emotions were a mile wide and an inch thick, however, as the cliche goes, their fervor didn't last very long.

Here's an important lesson for today as some of our friends get caught up in prophecies and frenzied worries like Edwards' brand of frightening and threatening spirituality. Such worries are not grounded in the positive faith and hope that represent constructive apocalyptic spirituality. Faith grounded in hope and love lasts. Faith rooted in fear often burns out, a victim of its own pessimism and negativity.

Edwards' vision of the End is also instructive for us today because he continued in America the European tradition of hate—where Protestants and Catholics leveled charges of the Antichrist against each other. This kind of labeling, as we have seen, distracts us from the core of personal renewal. Edwards preached to his parishioners that they should look within their own hearts for sin, but he fired them up by proclaiming Roman Catholicism and "popery" to be related to the Antichrist.

Edwards told his congregation they were a persecuted minority of saints locked in a cosmic struggle between good (represented by the Puritans) and evil (the Catholics) being played out within their own lives. "So Protestants oppose those who hold themselves to be the only true Church of God, who in the meantime are the church of the devil," Edwards wrote in a notebook of interpretations of the Book of Revelation which he worked on his whole life. He added later:

> But it is revenge on popery and antichristianism that [Protestant saints] desire, the destruction and ruin of that, either in the destruction or conversion of papists; this is what ought to be desired, that the proud and cruel enemies of the [Protestant] church, should be either converted or destroyed. And those times will be glorious when it shall be so; those times are to be wished for, wherein the saints shall destroy the beast....For [Catholic] priests are but the instruments of the devil; they work by his power. The whole of their religion is his contrivance, and it is by the subtilty and craft of the devil that they have thus deceived all nations....[I]t can't be better expressed than that the popish clergy have bewitched the nations.[3]

The United States: A Holy People

It's no surprise that American politicians built upon these traditions of faith and apocalypticism to paint national pride in religious terms. Remember, now, that constitutionalism was one of the ways people could take charge of their own lives, cast off the tyranny of the king, and declare themselves a new people reborn and destined for democratic greatness. If politicians are to be believed, Americans succeeded in making themselves their own special race of holy people.

The American Revolution tried to accomplish this goal. Revolutionaries used some apocalyptic imagery as they rallied around the "Don't tread on me!" slogan. Tapping into popular ideas, one American revolutionary specifically identified Great Britain as the beast of the Apocalypse. Another said that "the hero of civil and religious liberty" was actually the child born of the woman clothed in the sun. This hero was God's anointed one who was saved from the dragon and taken into heaven (Revelation 12). According to this American revolutionary, that child who was fighting British tyranny by slaying the beast of the Apocalypse was born on July 4, 1776.[4]

From the moments of our settling as colonies and our birth as a nation, therefore, Americans wanted to be living a life just like the millennium of peace and prosperity for which so many hoped. The American colonists and revolutionaries fought what some of them identified as a great battle between the forces and ideas of the good (democracy) and the persecution of the evil (tyranny). As we've seen, the Constitution codified religious ideals that had long been flowing through America's body, even though our country officially separates religion from civil government. Americans expanded their horizons and took over the continental United States under the popular cry of "Manifest Destiny." They believed they were destined by God to reach all the way from the Atlantic to the Pacific.

All of these examples, especially the idea of the child born of the woman clothed in the sun as having a birthday on the Fourth of July 1776, represent political and religious rhetoric at its most imaginative. But we must be careful in our time not to scoff at such notions from two hundred years ago at the same time that we are attracted—and distracted—by more recent versions in our own day. What we will find as we move along to look into our own most recent history of the twentieth century is that very often we do just that. We repeat the mistakes of the past even while we giggle at them.

The failure to learn the lessons of the past will be especially clear as we look at the history of elites who see themselves as the elect to be saved at the End and spared the tribulation of the Last Judgment. This idea is the "Rapture" which, if it doesn't come as quickly as some predict, will at least appear in our next chapter.

Notes

1. John Bartlett, *Familiar Quotations,* 14th ed., Emily Morison Beck, ed. (Boston: Little, Brown and Company, 1968), p. 412.
2. Douglas Robinson, *American Apocalypses: The Image of the End of the World in American Literature* (Baltimore: The Johns Hopkins University Press, 1985), p. xi.
3. Stephen J. Stein, ed., *Jonathan Edwards: Apocalyptic Writings* (New Haven: Yale University Press, 1977), pp. 99, 111, 122.
4. Arthur W. Wainwright, *Mysterious Apocalypse: Interpreting the Book of Revelation* (Nashville: Abingdon Press, 1993), pp. 168-169.

Chapter Four

The Meaning of the Millennium for Today

So far, we've seen many meanings of the End of the world in the family history of the Church. Some Christians saw the End only in terms of persecutions; many chose to withdraw from the world as a closed elite and wait for Jesus' Second Coming. Other Christians went on the defensive and labeled any of their enemies outside the Church (or within) as the Antichrist. Lost between these two meanings of the End was the moderate way of the Fathers: preparing through constant personal renewal.

But what does this history mean for us more immediately as we venture into the beginning of the third millennium? More specifically, it's time to ask how we can avoid the distracting parts of our history and embrace the Fathers' positive ideas on personal renewal which are repeated in Pope John Paul II's writings. The major lesson comes from the dangers of Catholic amnesia. If we were clunked on the head today and couldn't recognize our families, our jobs, or our past education, then we couldn't wake up tomorrow, kiss our families good-bye, and go off to work or school. In the same way, if Catholics don't know who Catholics were and what they did in the past, we can't be Catholics today or tomorrow. More specifically for our subject of apocalypticism, if we don't bear in mind the craziness that has been born out of ignorance and fear in our past, we risk repeating it now and in the future.

Rating the Rapture: A Look in the Mirror

Many of the important aspects of apocalypticism, especially the negative, come together in the recent history of religion and politics in the United States. We Christians have to be honest enough to look at ourselves in the mirror and admit this potent mix. We must emphasize personal renewal while others in our country simply continue those distracting "Woe is us!" and "The End is near!" prophecies as we enter the Church's third millennium. A good place to start this honest look in the mirror is with the idea of the Rapture.

Versions of the Rapture may be one of the most popular elements of apocalypticism in our own day in the United States. The idea of the Rapture has a long history that reaches back to the New Testament, including some of the earliest writings in the Church's history (1 Thessalonians 4:16-17; 2 Corinthians 12:2; Matthew 24:31,40-41; Luke 17:34-35). Basically, the Rapture is an interpretation of the End that predicts some people, because they are judged worthy, will be spared a great tribulation of suffering that will afflict those left behind.

Some will be taken, as the gospels say, and others left. The first group will be taken away (the Latin is *rapiemur*, which means "we shall be snatched away" or "we shall be carried off") to heaven, usually for seven years. It's as if these people will be on a big cloud in the sky, leaning over the sides to watch the second group—those left behind—fight it out in a battle of good versus evil. It's worth noting, of course, that Matthew 24:42 (the verse *right after* one of the scriptural passages often connected to the notion of some being taken away and others left) reminds us that we do not know when this will occur. But the message of Matthew 24:42 gets lost in the enticing possibility that we will be spared the supposed dangers and troubles of the End.

The Rapture has attracted a fair amount of attention in the United States since the middle of the nineteenth century. As recently as the 1970s one apocalyptic author predicted, "Our generation may well be the last before Christ returns to remove believers from the Earth."[1] The problem, of course, is that even if those who believe in a Rapture follow the warning that no one knows when this will occur, they are continuing that difficult tradition of naming themselves as the elect. If some apocalyptic leaders don't go this far, they still imply that people following particular beliefs and lifestyles have the best chance to be the elect.

Now comes the time to look at ourselves in the mirror. Viewed through the lessons of history, we can see that hanging on to the alleged promise of the Rapture is to embrace the same gnostic elitism of some in the early Church and those medieval Taborites on their isolated mountaintop in February, 1420. Like those elitists in the past, we are saying, "Hooray for us!" at the same time we are saying, "Go to hell!" quite literally. This "us versus them" is a sad reminder of the Catholic versus Protestant rhetoric we heard in Europe during the Reformations and later in America. If we are honest with ourselves in the mirror, we can see that this may be an element of apocalypticism, but it is not a very positive Christian attitude.

Still, the idea that some of us will be judged worthy and will be spared the tribulations of the End holds a very magnetic appeal, especially during periods of insecurity: economic, political, or social. When we are insecure and have questions, it's easy to be persuaded by someone who claims to have all the answers and offers security in the middle of confusion. This is why we must beware of the allure of the charming charlatan who promises the big answers to the big questions: When will the End come? How can we prepare and be ready for the End? How can we survive the End?

Such characters promise the answers, but deliver just one more updated version of the fundamentalism, paranoia, and fear that have typified the negative aspects of apocalypticism for almost twenty centuries. If these people are not rooted in the positive and personal elements of apocalyptic spirituality, they offer only empty promises.

Empty Promises that Can Catch Your Eye

How have Christians been enticed by these empty promises and programs for being worthy of the Rapture in the twentieth century? There are many examples—and with the unfiltered and unedited bulletin boards of the Internet, there will be many more. Authors have spent hundreds of pages illustrating and analyzing the most recent trends in apocalyptic readings of the United States and world affairs of the last several decades, so we won't go into the details they have already discovered. By taking a look at some of the more stereotypical and well-known apocalyptic promises and explanations of the twentieth century, however, we can help ourselves prepare for some of the prophecies to come, prophecies that will surely offer the same old empty promises even if they are dressed up in high-tech terms.

The most surprising element of apocalypticism in our own times is the return of fundamentalist, literal readings of the Book of Revelation and other scriptural passages that concern the End. We've had a century of careful research into how the Bible was written and the best ways that the Church offers for understanding the messages and lessons of the Bible. But people are still interested in the fundamentalist way of interpreting the Bible literally so the events of their day fit into scenarios of the End Times.

This literal effort is very familiar to us by now. As we've seen, some early Christians tried to identify the persecutions they suffered under the Roman Empire with the trials in the Book of Revelation. The advance of the Moslems and the role of the Jews were also fit into apocalyptic scenarios throughout the Middle Ages. Even though these were obviously wrong—we're all still here—modern-day versions of these literal interpretations persist.

Because fundamentalism has returned and is repeating previous trends, now is the perfect time to remember the history of the Church and to learn the lessons of the past. After all, if the identifications of events like the fall of the Roman Empire with biblical prophecies turned out to be incorrect, then why should we think versions of the same identifications in our own day will be correct? The answer: some people never learn. Chief among modern-day people who continue to repeat the mistakes of the past and fail to learn the lessons of Church history are writers who fit current events into their accounts of the End of the world. The fact that their books are best sellers should be troubling and indicates that the lessons of the past are indeed passing by unlearned.

In general, these literal interpretations and "prophecies," starting with the post-World-War-II era, depicted the Cold War as the battle between the forces of good/democracy (with the United States in the lead) and evil/communism (especially the Soviet Union and the People's Republic of China). The increased fears of nuclear war in the 1960s, 1970s, and 1980s obviously played right into such scenarios since countries controlled the technology to destroy the world many times over. But even with long-range missiles, modern-day fears of the End are not very different at their core from medieval fears that the world would come crashing down if crops failed, animals died, and family members starved to death.

In recent years, apocalyptic writers in the United States turned the economic uncertainty of the 1970s and the Mideast oil crisis into a sign that the Moslems were at it again. Others focused on the role of the Jews by placing tremendous emphasis on the state of Israel. Some of these writers saw the establishment of Israel in 1948 and the Israelis' capture of all of the city of Jerusalem in 1967 as signs that the End would come soon since the Jews were returning to their biblical homeland. And during the Persian Gulf War, some of the Christian-Jewish-Moslem ties were once more at work. America, which was allied with Israel, was called the Great Satan by Saddam Hussein, continuing similar imagery and rhetoric raised during the Iranian hostage crisis and the tensions between President Jimmy Carter and Iran's Ayatollah Khomeini. Americans, in turn, painted Hussein as the second coming of Hitler.

Even presidents have used this imagery. It's well documented that Ronald Reagan used religious and apocalyptic images. The most famous example occurred when he hinted that the Soviet Union was evil in his famous "Evil Empire" speech before the National Association of Evangelicals in 1983. President Reagan also alluded to the End in a statement he made to a lobbyist for the American-Israel Public Affairs Committee. As recounted in the

Jerusalem Post and then the *Washington Post*, the President is reported to have said:

> You know, I turn back to your ancient prophecies in the Old Testament and the signs foretelling Armageddon, and I find myself wondering if—if we're the generation that's going to see that come about. I don't know if you've read any of these prophecies lately, but believe me, they certainly describe the times we're going through.

Asked about these kinds of statements in a presidential debate in 1984, however, Reagan replied that no one knows for sure when Armageddon will come. During the debate on television, Reagan stated, "So, I have never seriously warned and said we must plan according to Armageddon."[2]

And the political appeals continue. Candidates for public office continue to mix religion with politics. To take just one example from many, when Texas Senator Phil Gramm ran for the Republican nomination for president in 1995, he included the following statement in a letter to the Christian Coalition's annual convention: "There's only one person who's ever lived who I would trust to impose values on America. And when He comes back, He won't need government to impose his values."[3]

Fascinated by the End

Why are people so fascinated with the End right now, especially in the United States? It might, in fact, have nothing to do with the millennium. After all, prophecies which did not mention the turning of the century or the millennium were cropping up several decades ago.

A number of historians, sociologists, psychologists, and other scholars link this fascination with the End, especially in the 1950s through the 1990s, with fears that nuclear war will obliterate the world, that overpopulation will lead to massive starvation, or that rapidly-increasing technology will simply use up the world's natural resources and leave people with nothing to eat or drink. In recent End-of-the-world scenarios, economic troubles are matched with versions of destruction that rely mainly on nuclear holocausts. Other observers of the history of apocalypticism notice an extreme fear of technology. Because some people distrust machines and computers that dominate our world, they shun the world by looking for the End. Among extremists, militarists advocate turning their backs on society, building bunkers, and waiting for the End with loaded rifles—not unlike those Taborites in the fifteenth century, David Koresh's Branch Davidians in Waco, Texas in 1993, and the followers of the Heaven's Gate cult in California in 1997 who took their own lives in the ultimate rejection of their bodies (which they called earthly "vehicles") and this world.

Though many scoff at these actions, there is obviously a market for the books and public discussion of the End; publishers and organizers keep the titles coming. One author, for example, wrote a survival guide that put the ultimate spin on the publishing world's "how to" books: *Christians Will Go Through the Tribulation: And How to Prepare For It.* Another writer combined technophobia and the economist's fear that we're overextending ourselves on credit by warning against "the 666 system." According to this author, the Antichrist and his followers are already marked in the bar codes and electromagnetic strips that decorate everything from our groceries and library books to our credit and ATM cards. At the End, Antichrist followers will have one credit card to do all of their transactions. (Talk about not leaving home without *that*!) This plan recommends that all Americans cut up these coded cards, stock up on gold and silver, and wait for the Rapture that will sweep them away.[4]

Perhaps just one example will show how the lessons of the past continue to go unlearned. A colleague mailed me a flyer for a series of workshops that discussed prophecies of the End in connection with the Year 2000. It was like looking at the mistakes of Church history in a few slick pages. The colorful brochure wondered if the Year 2000 would produce "World Peace or World Disaster?" It promised that I would "Discover the real truth about...The Mark of the Beast and Mysterious #666...The United States in Prophecy...The Future of America...Near Death Experiences."

The cover recounted a litany of modern troubles: "ethnic conflicts, worldwide instability, increased natural disasters, social unrest, rising crime, troubled families." But these are nothing compared to the tougher times ahead, the material warned. The program schedule went on to highlight some of the workshops to be offered: "Countdown to Eternity: Prophecy predicts the coming of a new world. You can be part of it"; "A World in Turmoil. Over 20 signs of Christ's Second Coming have been revealed; there is one left!"; and "The New Age Conspiracy: Psychic Phenomenon and the Real Truth About the End of Time. How to keep from being deceived in the days ahead."

Here, then, are modern versions of past actions in Church history. The program offers the truth behind mysteries like 666. It promises to interpret the prophecies of the Bible in terms of current events, especially America's role in the End Times. The organizers make us wonder if the Year 2000 will introduce world disaster or world peace—implicitly saying that it has to be one extreme or the other.

In apparent ignorance of the fact that historical events seemed to tumble one right after the other in centuries other than our own, the organizers foster the idea that our current times are the worst ever. They list the fall of the Berlin Wall along with conflicts in Africa, the Middle East, and the Balkans, noting ominously, "Some cosmic force seems to be pushing us toward a great catastrophe. We feel it...sense it deep within but are powerless to change it." They seem to forget Jesus' own caution in the gospels that there will be wars and rumors of wars among other calamities and prophecies that the Messiah had come, but that these will *not* be the End (Matthew 24 and 25, Mark 13, Luke 21).

To their credit, however, and perhaps in spite of themselves, the organizers do tap into the other, more positive tradition of personal renewal by offering a workshop called, "How to Find Personal Peace. The real answer to guilt, discouragement and low esteem" and another titled, "Alive at End Time: Living to the Fullest. How to break undesirable habits and transform your past."

To be fair to the audience attracted by this brochure, I admit that it's easy to be pushed off the proper track. Even when academics or teachers get together to discuss the history of apocalypticism, several end up saying, "Did you read that supermarket tabloid story about the four horsemen of the Apocalypse showing up in Arizona?" Once when I was meeting with other speakers to discuss our presentations at an upcoming conference on the Year 2000, we naturally fell into this pit, asking each other, "Did you hear the one about…?" Finally, the conference moderator warned us, "We're doing exactly what we're warning against!" That danger is always there.

To Speak About the End or Not to Speak: That Is the Question

People with lots of questions—and even those who should know better—are fascinated with this kind of material. Who wouldn't be attracted by the promise of answers to fascinating but mysterious questions? But the problem comes when prophets claim to have the answer to a question that even Jesus can't answer. No amount of arguing with such people is helpful. We simply waste our time in endless debates about scenarios and interpretations.

If others, including some Catholics, hold on to the belief that the calendar date and time of the End can indeed be calculated while we hold on to the truth that even Jesus doesn't know the End, there's no way to communicate. Two people with such fundamentally opposed principles simply can't meet.

However, there is a certain irony at work. What if we were to calmly point out to those who claim to have the final formula for the End that even Jesus doesn't know the date or time of the End? Couldn't we be accused of doing exactly what we criticize others of doing: having *the* answer?

So, we must ask ourselves whether we should engage modern-day apocalypticists in discussion or not. If we do, we risk being drawn into a debate using their terms and, almost by definition, implying that it is in fact possible to figure out the time of the End. This is what happened to the Jesuits arguing against the Protestants in the sixteenth and seventeenth centuries, as you'll recall.

In other words, by debating with modern-day apocalypticists we may legitimate their claim that the End can in fact be calculated. To those who read or hear such a debate, it can seem that all we are arguing about are the details. Again, an example from Church history is instructive. An eighth-century Spanish monk with the colorful name Beatus of Liébana carefully counted the number of years between biblical events. But immediately after writing down his figures, he reminded his readers:

> The time remaining to the world is uncertain to human investigation. Our Lord Jesus Christ rejected every kind of question on this matter when he said: "It does not belong to you to know the times or the moments which the Father has put in his own power" (Acts of the Apostles 1:7); or again: "No one knows the day nor the hour—neither the angels of heaven, nor the Son, but only the Father" (Mark 13:32).

Beatus went on to stress that time in the mind of God may be very different to time as we measure it in hourglasses, wrist watches, or digital alarm clocks. What's a day to God?

> Because he said "day and hour," sometimes they are to be taken for general time spans, sometimes to be understood directly. You should know in truth that the world will end in 6,000 years; but whether these years are to be completed or shortened is known only to God.[5]

Catholics must bear in mind, then, that an acceptable answer to the key question, "When will the End come?" is "We don't know. But we *do* know that it can't be figured out if Jesus himself doesn't know." Catholics should simply and rationally heed Jesus' caution that even he doesn't know when the End will occur. That may be the best way to offer some calm, peaceful wisdom without getting into an argument.

Therefore, one way of demonstrating that speculation will always fail is to point out how past predictions, especially reading the signs of the political times, were always wrong. Teach others the lessons of Church history, then, to avoid repeating the mistakes of the past. People calculated certain dates for the End—and no End followed. Rome fell—no End. Three popes—no End. Protestants and Catholics saw the Antichrist in each other—no End. Hitler was defeated—no End. Communism collapsed—no End.

Apocalyptic Algebra Just Doesn't Add Up

Another way of presenting the Catholic attitude is actually to engage in what may be called apocalyptic algebra: using predictions of time from the Bible and calculating the End by counting up days, weeks, months, and years to fit into a certain End date. To go against a theme that's been running throughout this book, therefore, let's indulge for a moment in some apocalyptic algebra just to make a point.[6]

As we've already mentioned, this is tricky stuff since we can easily end up playing on someone else's turf. But it is sometimes effective to show that speculation about the End is simply a children's game that anyone can win or lose. It's especially a game when we hold on to the rules—in this case the words of Scripture—rigidly and literally until we need to change them. But the point of thinking about the End is not to show how clever we are; it's not about winning and losing. It's about looking to the future with hope and in a good state of personal readiness.

Again, Church history is our teacher. Many predictions of the End center on apocalyptic algebra as we've described it. However, it's extremely easy to demonstrate that this is not an exact science. And if you disprove one version of events and timing, then others immediately come under suspicion. Here's an example.

Consider one of the most well-known sources of prophecy about the End: the Book of Daniel. In several places the Book of Daniel mentions time; Chapter 12, for example, discusses a period of warfare and tribulation accompanied by a time of testing and refinement at the End. According to Daniel 12:11, this period will be precisely 1,290 days. The very next verse, however, Daniel 12:12 states that whoever perseveres 1,335 days will be blessed.

So what happens during the forty-five days in between? Essentially, writers considering the Book of Daniel had to cover this apparent contradiction somehow. They eventually and creatively came up with the idea that these forty-five days would be a time when people who had yet to repent would get one last chance to make up for their sins. This period of time was usually known as the "refreshment of the saints." It was set between the end of the Antichrist's reign (predicted as forty-two months, or about 1,260 days, in Revelation 13:5) and the Last Judgment. In one version or another, the "refreshment of the saints" was very popular in the Middle Ages.[7]

Surprisingly, Saint Jerome, one of the Fathers who actually cautioned *against* a literal reading of Scripture, was the person who first came up with the idea. After him, writers in the Middle Ages elaborated on what would happen during these forty-five days. Some said the Jews and Moslems would be converted to Christianity while others predicted a general rise in spirituality and faith.

To view this negatively, we can say that here is another example of some very imaginative minds at work; if these ideas of the End did not fit the Scripture, they'd make them fit any way they could.

The fact that so many writers spent a great deal of effort trying to understand Saint Jerome's interpretation of the forty-five days— some even saw it as more like forty-five years and explained in detail why—reminds us once more of how calculations like these can distract us from positive apocalyptic spirituality. If we spend all of our time on these interpretations, we are in danger of missing Saint Jerome's point about "refreshing" and renewing ourselves in preparation for meeting God.

But the example of the development of the idea of the "refreshment of the saints" can also be viewed positively when engaging modern apocalypticists who are trying to read Scripture literally. First, we can show them that adding to Scripture in this way actually detracts from their own principle that Scripture alone holds the key to dating the time of the End. For if Scripture holds the key, why the need to add to Scripture to date the End? Second, and much more charitably, we can point out a principle of the Fathers at work: their message that we should always be ready for the End, whenever it comes. In this manner, we can engage others without alienating them. At the same time, we share our Catholic faith: if Jesus himself doesn't know the time of the End, who are we to try to figure it out? Instead, we can spend our time much more profitably.

John Paul II: Crossing the Threshold with Hope

Here, then, is yet one more example of how we can do what the Catholic faith has challenged us to do from the New Testament through the documents of Vatican II: to be "in" this world without being "of" it. If we have faith that God knows what God is doing, if we have hope that the End will be a wonderful event, and if we know our Church history, we can engage in an apocalyptic dialogue without being sucked into the craziness. How, then, does Pope John Paul II ask us to prepare for the Church's third millennium?[8]

Almost since the first moments of his pontificate, John Paul II began pointing to the new millennium. However, this does not mean that he is an apocalyptic visionary in the mold of Joachim of Fiore in the Middle Ages or any other writer who tried to calculate the End and put a date on it. John Paul II sees the beginning of the new millennium as an anniversary. In his central document about the coming of the twenty-first century, *Tertio Millennio Adveniente* (*On the Coming Third Millennium*, #1316), John Paul II explained that in the history of the Jews and the Church a jubilee year was a joyful year of reconsidering where you stand with God, a year of special blessings and pardons, a year of healing old wounds and starting fresh.

But don't read anything more into the Pope's use of the Year 2000 as a jubilee. There's no hint in his writings that he thinks the new millennium will be the End. For him, the beginning of the twenty-first century is simply a natural, logical place to pause and think about what's gone before us so we can move ahead—not unlike going on a retreat or having a long talk with God when we turn forty or fifty or when we become a parent, make a career move, or retire.

John Paul II mentioned the Year 2000 in his very first encyclical, *Redemptor Hominis* (*Redeemer of Man*), issued less than six months after his election as pope. In the first paragraph, he noted even then—March 1979—that we were getting close to the Year 2000, but he made no predictions. What he did do, however, and this is very significant, was tap into the Fathers' idea of personal renewal in Christ. This is one of the keys to positive apocalyptic spirituality for John Paul II, as when he teaches:

> At this moment it is difficult to say what mark that year will leave on the face of human history or what it will bring to each people, nation, country and continent, in spite of the efforts already being made to foresee some events. For the Church,...it will be the year of a great Jubilee...[which] will recall and reawaken in us in a special way our awareness of the key truth of faith which Saint John expressed at the beginning of his gospel: "The Word became flesh and dwelt among us" (*Redemptor Hominis*, #1).

In that encyclical and many times since, the Pope calls the period of preparation an Advent—yet another reminder of a time of personal renewal and repentance in preparation for a great event. In this case, John Paul II's use of the word "Advent" is especially helpful because we link Advent with Christmas—that moment when Jesus came into the world as an individual human being. Naturally, we can use this image to focus on our own individuality and not waste our time with big conceptions of the End of the world.

More specifically, the Pope sees Vatican II as an Advent because it laid down a program for Catholics to follow:

> The best preparation for the new millennium, therefore, can only be expressed in a renewed commitment to apply, as faithfully as possible, the teachings of Vatican II to the life of every individual and of the whole Church. It was with the Second Vatican Council that, in the broadest sense of the term, the immediate preparations for the Great Jubilee of the Year 2000 were really begun (*Tertio Millennio Adveniente*, #20).

A good way to ground our faith for the challenges of a new millennium would be to reread, or maybe read for the first time, the documents of Vatican II and the texts that flowed out from the Council's actions.

But how is John Paul II *unlike* those writers and leaders who focus on negative apocalypticism? How does he, by contrast, continue the positive aspects of personal renewal that the Fathers of the Church urge on us while others scan the skies and the headlines for signs of the End? First, John Paul II specifically focuses on individual reform. "Everything ought to focus on the primary objective of the Jubilee: the strengthening of faith and of the witness of Christians," he writes in *Tertio Millennio Adveniente* (#42). "It is therefore necessary to inspire in all the faithful a true longing for holiness, a deep desire for conversion and personal renewal in a context of ever more intense prayer and of solidarity with one's neighbor, especially the most needy." He also tells us that we should look at the history of the Church for signs of injustice, intolerance, violence, and lack of faith. The focus, then, is on ourselves.

A second lesson is related to the first. Pope John Paul II calls for dialogue with the world's great religions, especially Judaism and Islam, and for dialogue among all Christian groups. This is a direct lesson from Church history. Catholics, you'll recall, spent a fair amount of time accusing Jews and Moslems of being the henchmen of the Antichrist when thinking about the End. Catholics and

Protestants lobbed charges of evil and corruption at each other. In all cases, we can see that Christians distracted themselves from looking within while making charges against others.

As noted before, an "us versus them" mentality is clearly destructive and leads to charges of self-righteousness when Christians start calling Jews and Moslems "wrong" and "damned." It's even sadder, perhaps, when some Catholics declare themselves "the true Church" while labeling other Catholics an evil "them." We're asked to remember what the Fathers taught us: to look within our own hearts first. Only then can we share the Good News in faith and charity.

Third, and coming from the first two, the Pope warns against the modern-day gnostic elites who see themselves as the elect and others as damned. In the encyclical *Dominum et Vivificantem* (*Lord and Giver of Life*, #54) from 1986, John Paul II wrote, "The great Jubilee to be celebrated at the end of this Millennium and at the beginning of the next ought to constitute a powerful call to all those who 'worship God in spirit and truth.'" Notice that he calls to everybody, not just a few. He does not state that the gates of salvation and Rapture are already closed. Rather, he offers an open invitation.

Fourth, while he names the Year 2000 as a Jubilee, he also tells us to go beyond simple ideas of time as a marker of events. Jesus, after all, was probably born around 6 or 4 B.C., but does that matter? Yes—but only if you are reading the Bible literally and missing the importance of the Incarnation whenever it occurred.

> Creation is thus completed by the Incarnation and since that moment is permeated by the powers of the Redemption, powers which fill humanity and all creation....For we must go beyond the historical dimension of the event considered in its surface value....[W]e cannot limit ourselves to the two thousand years which have passed since the birth of Christ. We need to go further back, to embrace the whole of the action of the Holy Spirit even before Christ—from the beginning, throughout the world, and especially in the economy of the Old Covenant (*Dominum et Vivificantem*, #52-53).

The meaning of the Incarnation has to be understood in terms of what the Holy Spirit has been doing for us since the beginning of time. What God has done for us in the past teaches us about what God is doing for us in the present.

But the meaning of the millennium turns our thoughts to the future, too. This fact brings our attention to the fifth way John Paul II is urging a different and positive path: a hopeful approach to the future. As we've seen, many apocalyptic movements and writers focused on the destruction to come at the End. Even if they promised salvation afterwards (or during, if we were to be spared in the Rapture), the language was always foreboding and threatening. That negative message stretches across the years from the legends of the Antichrist through Jonathan Edwards' sermons and Hal Lindsey's books, including one with the unnerving title, *The 1980s: Countdown to Armageddon*.

John Paul II focuses on optimism, not pessimism. He is not, however, blind to the sad aspects of Church history he calls us to study. In fact, he's been a leader in identifying times when the Church has acted with little charity or justice. He knows personally many of the events that have made the twentieth century a century of sorrows. But he doesn't dwell on these aspects.

Instead, John Paul II looks to the future with hope. As he told the United Nations in 1995, "The tears of this century have prepared the ground of a new springtime of the human spirit." We are entering a new phase of history, he continually points out, and there's no cause to worry. "Be not afraid!" were some of the first words he said in public on the day of his election as pope. He has repeated them ever since.

In short, positive apocalyptic spirituality like that offered by the Fathers, carried through by some Catholics in the history of the Church, and championed today by John Paul II, is everything that negative spirituality is not. Positive apocalyptic spirituality is constructive, not destructive. It offers the image of the End as a reminder for personal reform and criticism that is given to correct someone. Positive apocalyptic spirituality does not chastise people or drive them to anguish or fear. It focuses on the ultimate victory of the cross, not on battles. It is not dark and gloomy, but a bright light shining before all. It avoids self-righteousness and a persecution complex that drives the persecuted to become persecutors. It sees that literal readings of Scripture lend themselves to distortion, misreading, and outright error. While negative apocalyptic spirituality diverts our attention and energy into unproductive channels, as Saint Augustine warned over fifteen hundred years ago, positive apocalyptic spirituality focuses on inner reflection, change, and growth in faith, hope, and love.

There is no cause for fear, but plenty of reason to trust in the Lord. "Be not afraid!" may be our best motto, then, as we enter the third millennium with hope.

Notes

1. Quoted in Arthur W. Wainwright, *Mysterious Apocalypse: Interpreting the Book of Revelation* (Nashville: Abingdon Press, 1993), p. 84.
2. These and other similar statements of President Reagan are recounted at length and analyzed in Stephen D. O'Leary, *Arguing the Apocalypse: A Theory of Millennial Rhetoric* (New York: Oxford University Press, 1994), pp. 180-183 and pp. 272-276.
3. *The New York Times*, September 23, 1995.
4. Both examples may be found in Bernard McGinn, *Antichrist: Two Thousand Years of the Human Fascination with Evil* (San Francisco: HarperSanFrancisco, 1994), p. 261.
5. McGinn, *Visions of the End: Apocalyptic Traditions in the Middle Ages* (New York: Columbia University Press, 1979), p. 78.
6. Even Saint Augustine, while cautioning against calculating the End, provided a scenario of the world as progressing or "aging" in six stages which many writers later used to date the End.
7. For a full account of the development of this idea, from which this small sketch is drawn, see Robert E. Lerner, "Refreshment of the Saints: The Time after Antichrist as a Station for Earthly Progress in Medieval Thought," *Traditio* 32 (1976), pp. 97-144.
8. For a more complete explanation of John Paul II's teaching on this topic, see Avery Dulles, "John Paul II and the Advent of the New Millennium," *America* (December 9, 1995), pp. 9-15. Several of Fr. Dulles' quotations of the Pope's statements and his insights into them are treated in this section.

For Further Reading

Paul J. Alexander. *The Byzantine Apocalyptic Tradition*. Berkeley: University of California Press, 1985.

Ruth H. Bloch. *Visionary Republic: Millennial Themes in American Thought, 1756-1800*. Cambridge: Harvard University Press, 1985.

John J. Collins. *The Apocalyptic Imagination: An Introduction to the Jewish Matrix of Christianity*. New York: Crossroad, 1987.

Brian E. Daley. *The Hope of the Early Church: A Handbook of Patristic Eschatology*. Cambridge: Cambridge University Press, 1991.

Theodore T. Daniels. *Millennialism: An International Bibliography*. New York: Garland, 1992.

Richard Kenneth Emmerson. *Antichrist in the Middle Ages: A Study of Medieval Apocalypticism, Art, and Literature*. Seattle: University of Washington Press, 1981.

___ and Bernard McGinn, eds. *The Apocalypse in the Middle Ages*. Ithaca: Cornell University Press, 1993.

Robert C. Fuller. *Naming the Antichrist: The History of an American Obsession*. New York: Oxford University Press, 1995.

Andrew C. Gow. *The Red Jews: Antisemitism in an Apocalyptic Age, 1200-1600*. Leiden: E.J. Brill, 1994.

Nathan O. Hatch. *The Sacred Cause of Liberty: Republican Thought and the Millennium in Revolutionary New England*. New Haven: Yale University Press, 1977.

John Paul II. *Tertio Millennio Adveniente*. Boston: St. Paul Books & Media, 1994.

Bernard McGinn. *Antichrist: Two Thousand Years of the Human Fascination with Evil*. San Francisco: HarperSanFrancisco, 1994.

___, ed. *Apocalyptic Spirituality*. New York: Paulist Press, 1979.

___. *Visions of the End: Apocalyptic Traditions in the Middle Ages*. New York: Columbia University Press, 1979.

W.W. Meissner. *Thy Kingdom Come: Psychoanalytic Perspectives on the Messiah and the Millennium*. Kansas City: Sheed & Ward, 1995.

Stephen D. O'Leary. *Arguing the Apocalypse: A Theory of Millennial Rhetoric*. New York: Oxford University Press, 1994.

Marjorie Reeves. *The Influence of Prophecy in the Later Middle Ages: A Study in Joachimism*. Oxford: Clarendon Press, 1969.

Michael J. St. Clair. *Millenarian Movements in Historical Context*. New York: Garland, 1992.

Arthur W. Wainwright. *Mysterious Apocalypse: Interpreting the Book of Revelation*. Nashville: Abingdon Press, 1993.